ATTICA DIARY

ATTICA DIARY

William R. Coons

STEIN AND DAY/*Publishers*/New York

B
Coo

To all those people, too numerous to mention, who made it seem possible. May the ones still in soon be out. May the ones still out remain that way. May the rest have found the peace they deserve.

MARCH, 1970

"You don't know me," she said. "You don't know me."

Her name was Justice, and she was right—I didn't. I had always thought I loved her, too—her generous bosom, her round cheeks, the smoothness of her marble skin, the shape of her arm, the taste of her alabaster kiss as it caught fire in the sunlight.

But she was a whore, like the rest. She wore dark robes during the day and sneaked through the streets at night. If you followed her long enough, she might make you a proposition. If you followed her too long, you'd find out she was just part of a ring—the one tightening around your neck.

By the time you're barely able to breathe, you've learned what Justice is. But by then, you've had your fill of her. You wouldn't even spit on her grave.

The day in County Jail that they let me have a letter from my mother I knew it was all over. The hacks were being kind. They knew I'd made a fool of them somehow, but they didn't know how. All they knew was, this shmuck who thought he was smart was going to get it up the ass.

So I didn't have much hope on sentencing day. That was good, because actually you're not supposed to have any. No more than your lawyer allows you, which is pretty close to that. Next to none.

He comes out of the judge's chambers like a maid-in-waiting from her Queen's royal toilet. The secrets he knows he will never reveal. They're going to hang this guy, I know he's thinking, because he screwed too many people. He screwed the D.A., he screwed the hacks in the

Safety Building, he screwed just about everybody including his wife, and now he thinks he's going to get a break. I hope they break it off. But I'll manage to be consoling. I'll tell him that's life, or something. I wish to hell they wouldn't give me these kinds of cases. I didn't go to law school to jerk off in Criminal Court, either. Oh, fuck it.

Nice lawyer. Nice young kid, clean-shaven, well dressed, conservative all-around, the judge is thinking. He should go far if he plays the game right. But so many of them start out like that. And so few of them stay that way. You really can't trust a lawyer nowadays, and everybody knows it.

But he took this case just a little bit to heart, which is just a little bit too far to take any of these cases. All of these people should be off the streets, and he should know it. Especially if they can't afford to pay. In prison they can at least contribute to the state.

Here's a man with a college education, a wife and two kids, and fucking around with LSD. A teacher, too. Well, a peek at the inside of a prison ought to teach him something.

But I'm thinking I can't stand this. They know what they're going to do, and they've known it all along. The eight months' jail time was a waste, there's not a chance of getting Time Served or even probation. The Probation officer was a Catholic, and this guy's a Christian. Which makes him think he's God, which is almost on a par with being a Catholic. But not quite. A Catholic has the advantage of knowing God's mind in advance. This guy doesn't have any mind at all, and that's what fucked the P.O. up. This guy has spent most of his life in front of a mirror, brushing back his graying temples. He had them when he was five and used to wear his mother's dresses around. They all thought that was cute. So did he, evidently, because the habit cropped up again later in life. God, this makes me sick to my guts . . .

The wife hasn't shown up.

That sounds like the first sentence of a bad novel. It can't be, though. Let's start it over:

She hasn't shown up.

No, no; that's too melodramatic—besides, somebody already tried it, and it got rejected.

Well, at least I'm able to write. They haven't broken my fingers yet. I hear they do that in the metal shop. I hear the machines are *bad* in there. I hear guys going there every day who thought they were going to be assigned to the hospital, to the kitchen, to the outside gangs, to the North Pole. But they're all going to the metal shop, and I'm next.

I can't.

God, I can't do that, and I won't. I've worked in too many factories, and I'm not going to end up in this one for twenty-five cents a day. And they're talking about striking and about that being the beginning of the whole thing, the way the Riot jumps off.

The Riot. Christ, I'm inside a movie, this is somebody else's dream, I didn't want any part of it.

I saw it all before. I saw this place, the bricks, the arches, the fantastic columns in the mess hall, the Romanesque architecture, the clerestory, the terrazzo floors. It's nothing but a gigantic shithouse. But why this sense of *déjà vu?* I've never been in prison before—or have I? We should go into that, but my head aches so bad now I can hardly write. How do you get an aspirin around here?

Oh, God, *I can't* . . .

One thing you can do in here is sleep.

Sure. It helps if you're half dead, though. These must be migraines; they were giving me Darvon in County Jail, three times a day, and here you can't even get an aspirin when you need one. One more headache like that and I'm gone, I can't stand that.

The doctor is frightening. He looks at you with one eye, the other pointed toward the ceiling, like an undertaker appraising the condition of a corpse. As soon as you open your mouth, he feels insulted—Dead Men don't speak; what's the meaning of this!

"You can't have that here," he sneers when I tell him about the Darvon. "This isn't County Jail—you've got *Drugs* on your record!"

Drugs. Dangerous Drugs. *Possession of a Dangerous Drug in the Third Degree.* What is a dangerous drug? All drugs are dangerous, including the coffee they serve in the mess hall. Things seem to be swimming in it, the kind of life you'd find in a small stagnant pond.

The mess hall. Every trip to that place takes on the quality of a nightmare. It has to be seen to be believed. I've seen it, but I still can't believe it—a cavern measureless but full of men. Shouting, talking, barely containing the riot within. They let it all out here, vocally at least—conversations being held three and four tables across. And the guards stand silently by with sticks, waiting for a false move.

At least my headache's down. I hope it stays down because my back's starting in again, and the only thing this therapeutic brace is doing is helping me to stand up. It's a wonder they let me have it, with the metal stays. But nobody is going to dig their way out of this grave, and they know it.

"We've never lost a man" is their motto. They never found one, either.

I can't do much more than jot here; it's too much waiting to see where they're going to assign me.

I won't take the metal shop. That's where all the horror stories seem to be coming from. Lost fingers, mangled arms. I need these fingers to write. I'm a writer. I know I'm a writer because I'm writing. Logic? Sanity?

Sweet Jesus, help me keep my head from falling off in this place!

About the sense of *déjà vu*. Incredible, but I heard as good an explanation for it as any.

Out in the yard, Diz said: "It's the vibrations from this place. You don't know it, but you tuned in to them some time or other. Dig, some of the old-timers in here, they take trips. Ask 'em. They been here umpteen years, and they know they ain't going nowhere, but they'll tell you at night they's going out of their bodies, man; leaving them behind and going to all sorts of places out there."

That's crazy, of course. But here the crazy is the sane. Yet I feel this fantastic pile of Romanesque bricks *did* haunt me, I *did* have a dream, long ago; I couldn't have been more than eighteen or nineteen, and I woke up in a cold, delirious sweat, having had one of those nightmares whose exquisite detail etches itself on your mind in a way that casual reality seldom can. I dreamed of the arches, the stone columns, the sea of dark faces in the high-ceilinged Romanesque mess hall, the bars and the green-walled cells and the rivet heads, sealing you in . . .

Edgar Allan Poe stuff again.

God.

There's nothing to do in Reception except write, sleep, go to the yard and play cards, or think. I dread each day.

Reception's in A-Block, and a block in this case means just about that—forty-two cells to a gallery, two galleries to a tier, three tiers to a block—a sort of steel and brick beehive. Geometrical boredom from the inside, and from

12

the outside the appearance of a barred and oversize mausoleum, perhaps: cold storage, a factory for the near-dead. It works with routine precision, ruthless efficiency. It's lock-in or lineup, lock-in or lineup, three times a day for meals, once or twice for yard.

Meanwhile they're working on your papers downstairs, rearranging your life story to conform to the evidence which now defines you as a criminal, an enemy of society, and if this place doesn't make you feel like a nonperson, nothing will. Lining up naked for physicals in the dispensary, the phrase "human cattle" keeps running through my mind.

The thinking's the worst. There must be some way to stop it. I can't stand my thoughts, they feel like broken razor blades, churning through my brain. Sleep is a blessing; in a way it's good I feel so sick, because there's no trouble sleeping—I could do it all day. Except I know I'll wake up eventually—there's the rub.

What we have here is a problem in consciousness. How would Mailer have handled it? I mean, if he ever stopped bullshitting people and actually did something to get himself in prison. Like write an honest book.

I suppose I could write like Mailer, but the long rolling sentence wouldn't be tight enough with the fear in this place. All paranoia terminates here. Every time you go to the mess hall, you wonder how it feels to have your throat slashed.

The blacks are angry. They ought to be. Most of them got railroaded worse than I did. All you have to do is take one look inside here and you know what's wrong with this society.

Everything.

At night you hear the shotguns go off around the wall. Target practice.

It's coming and they know it.

Day breaks over the roof of D-Block across the way
—a bloody red sun. Woke up early—before the first
bell, even. Today maybe they'll send me somwhere. The
school if I'm lucky. Kenny, the three-time loser who beat
a multiple-offender rap, says the school's in the bag. He
says his friend over there in D-Block runs it and put
me on the list my first day inside the wall. But it's been
a week now and no call-up, except for a test to prove I
could read.

Maybe I flunked it. Where my mind's at, anything is
possible. Reality shifts like sand in a windstorm, but
the cold steel and red brick seem as permanent as Cheops'
Tomb.

You can get poetic about the sun in here—it's the
only thing you can see that's natural. And the sky, of
course. It's a wonder they didn't build a dome over the
entire complex and paint more bricks and bars on it,
ending once and for all any illusion about being a child
of the universe. About being anything but a sewer rat,
skulking among the ruins of a civilization.

From the outside it looks like an Alice in Wonder-
land castle, or perhaps a leftover prop from the last production of *The Wizard of Oz*. Smooth, sloping gray
walls, steepled orange-roofed turrets at regular intervals,
but I didn't get to see the whole thing on the day they
brought me up, just the outthrust vee of the main gate.
The wall looked enormously high as I leaned against it,
still shackled, for yet another frisk.

"Ain't this a bitch," Willie said, grinning. His gold

tooth gleamed from his mahogany face, the only bright spot in the day.

All the boys from Syracuse were there in Reception, including some who had been sent up as much as a week or ten days before. There were more coming. Syracuse has taken to Law and Order the way a duck takes to oil slicks. It's choking in the slime. It might never see the light of day again, the political pollution count's so high.

But neither might we—all us dead bodies over which the D.A. got reelected. Fatten up the body count is the directive, so the voters will know just who's winning the War on Crime. If you napalm a few friendly villages in the process, what's the difference? An ash in the wind. We want action, we need *convictions, convictions . . . !*

Smile when the man snaps the camera, son. It's your first trip upstate and we want to remember you warm. In here you'll burn like a flame. Only the flame will be low—so low you won't know it's there, and it won't keep your hands and feet from freezing on those cold winter nights when the hack comes along and takes away your extra blanket. We get weather up here, you know—Ice Station Zebra action, but don't expect no atomic subs to come up from under and save your ass, YOU GODDAMNED CRIMINAL!

Now, take it easy, son; we still got the other side to play, the one where Tommy falls in love with the pinball machine and takes it home with him—do you know what he gets? THIRTY YEARS, son, under the laws of New York State, 'cause we don't go for that kind of thing up here, see? I mean the people don't cotton to those outside hustlers, you shouldda stayed in Noo Yawk! Resta the niggers down there, they wouldn't pay no mind to your action, but we run a *clean* community, see? Don't 'llow no *outside agitators*, we take care of our own right fine. Now I know you lived here awhile, but the fact is you also lived down there, which makes you part nigger, understand? Anyone been down there, he turns part nigger. Thinks he can go downtown and drink and smoke that shit with the niggers up here, but the niggers up here they know their place and they ain't about to tolerate any more than it takes to see what kind of scratch you're totin', either. Yessir, we got us some good niggers up here . . .

Now, what I want is for you to bend over and show me your asshole. We got information a nigger's been up there—that true? We got information your problem's sexual, which is what you get for hangin' around them Noo Yawk niggers. Okay, don't want to talk, huh? Okay —throw him in the clam, Sam!

Anything worse than a nigger, it's a nigger-lover! I want it down in his jacket he's Uncooperative. Maybe even Dangerous. Guess I've looked up enough assholes to know when a man's Uncooperative and Dangerous, hey, Sam?

The worst part about the gig is the way you keep reviewing your life. They know about that. What other purpose is there behind all this except psychological torture? The physical is nothing—the constant threat of it is something. But beyond that, it's the idea of falling into a pit so vile the stink will never get out of your nostrils. It will cling to the walls and bury itself in the protoplasm and molecular structure of nonindefinitely renewable cells.

Why did I take acid? That's the first question they want you to ask. The first of many, and it's all got to end up in the same place for everyone: *Why was I born?*

That's the only reason not to commit suicide. The final stage in the loser's game, the one that's been set up for me since I realized I wasn't even a Jew; I am merely White Trash. There's no excuse for White Trash. God's promise fell on all White Protestants; to have rejected it is a sin beyond redemption.

That makes me worse than a nigger. There's some excuse for a nigger, because he started out as a low form of life, and you can't expect anything from that—right? A Jew is a little better. He can get through Harvard without much trouble, and if he keeps his nose clean, maybe they'll let him take a ride through the Pacific and sniff a few Jap assholes.

Then, of course, there's Irishmen. If an Irishman can stay sober long enough to shoot a pistol, we'll put a uniform on him and let him keep the streets safe for General Motors.

Bile. It's really not me writing this, it's this prison,

what I see here. What I see here is what you're supposed to see during the worst type of psychedelic hallucinations. It's what Dante tried to see and almost made it. But he was a Catholic Puritan—he never even jerked off. He made poetry out of wet dreams.

Chaucer was something else. He made people out of plastic nativity scenes. He was a better Catholic than any of them. The kind you could have a drink with and know he wouldn't fart downwind. He never finished his poem, either . . .

What about Socrates? He outlived them all. He screwed them all, too. By the time he drank the juice of the root, he was finished. There were no more philosophical questions to be asked.

The tree of Life. What happened to it? Whose ax buried itself to the very roots? Why have I become a ninety-year-old paralytic? With only enough fear left in him to crawl to the commode? I don't want to curse God.

I won't curse God!

They gave us earphones today so we can plug in to the institutionally censored radio in our cells.

Senator McCarthy is still making statements. He ought to hear them over these earphones. He'd suck shit to get away from them. If I hadn't joined his "organization," I might not have had my phone tapped. If I hadn't had my phone tapped, I might still be with my kids. But who will believe that?

Who would believe the suck-hole of Syracuse, where joining an organization that poses the possibility of the salvation of the United States means going out to a lonely farm among lonely people and watching them trying sadly to freak out, some way or other? Who would believe that collecting names for a full-page ad in the Syracuse *Herald-Journal* means twenty-four-hour surveillance by the

FBI? Who would believe it then, and who will believe it now?

Who would believe they'd take a guy doing his last month of parole and threaten him with a violation if he didn't set you up? Who would believe the cops had been following you since Skidmore College, when a frustrated alcoholic wreck of a would-be writer back from his last possible fellowship marked you down for assassination when he finally learned the game was headhunting and turned you in for rumors of smoking pot with one of the students? Who would believe you didn't even fuck her but went home and told your wife you were losing your mind in this funky little nowhere town?

Now listen, you asshole—who would even give the slightest damn?

Maybe your mother.

But she's dying in a state mental institution.

Today's the day, I feel it. Now I dread moving. In A-Block yard, a cross-section of what's beyond; the "interior," three more identical blocks, but it's forbidding, it's like going a little deeper into the crypt. The transient block has its own little horrors, the pneumatic cell locks going off like pistols down the line, ten at a time, or sometimes the hacks run them off like machine-gun fire.

I'm afraid, I guess—of this place and everything in it. But worse than that, of the mind that can conceive of all this. Rumor has it the joint was designed by a female architect. That may be a bit of romanticism on the part of inmates—then again, it may be true. It's certainly conceivable. Laid out like a medieval fortress, but also a monastery. The interior is divided up into four yards, one for each block, connected by "tunnels" which converge at a central point called Times Square.

It's a geometric maze, a human cyclotron, a cloud chamber of the mind. It smells of old ancient crimes, the rack and the wheel. Of human misery concealed, neglected, forgotten. Last night a scream echoed across the courtyard from deep in the bowels of the monster out there. Three times the cry was heard. No one along the gallery said anything. We just lay there, listening.

It wasn't mentioned in the morning, either. The weather has been bad, a combination of cold rain and slush, and it's almost June. A moviemaker couldn't have manufactured a better climatic setting. A half hour in the yard and you're shivering inside your gray prison uniform, the threadbare coat they finally issued.

Spiritual death.

We must not speak of such things in here. In here the Voice of Silence reigns. Through these halls pass those who have lost their voices completely. The lame, the deaf, the dumb, the halt, the blind. But blindness is a quality that can only be measured in relation to soul.

In here there are many lost souls. In here there are those who couldn't steal a nickel without the help of a kindergarten teacher. Those who write English as though it were a foreign language. Those who have learned to speak in the streets, and their voices smell like burned rubber.

Rubber souls, doing a long stretch. Victims of insurance-company miscalculations. Dogs, who barked up the wrong tree . . .

In here there are faces carved by a Master Artist who lost his mind and substituted a misshapen sense of reality.

In here there are people the world didn't want. Not around, at least, where they could be seen. For these are the living secrets of their own souls, the ones they hide from themselves . . .

The food tastes lovely. The only problem is eating it. After County Jail, any food tastes lovely. I lost fifteen pounds and learned the meaning of the word "fast." It means to do without, in preference to what they're serving. It means to find out how good a glass of water can feel at three o'clock in the morning. When the hack makes his rounds and stabs you in the eyes with his Boy Scout Laser Flashlight. The motherfuckers. They were sending in Wheaties tops for a Better Deal when they were five. Now look at them.

Civil Servants. My God, I should have taken the test. It's the one way to bury yourself in this society without having to pay for the funeral.

The whole idea of keeping a diary is absurd. What does it prove? Whose thoughts are so private he wouldn't depart with them in a minute for nothing more than the sake of a good conversation?

But you can't get that in here, evidently. All you can do is hope for some relief in the monotony, and your words are just as fake as the next man's. Even in here it's keeping up the image that counts. And nobody's playing Bogart anymore except for one or two madmen, and they're wearing uniforms—their own kind of invisibility.

The hacks in the mess hall especially strike me as rather confused Hollywood extras. The scene has gotten out of hand and they know it. But they don't know how to react to it except with the same tired stereotypes that have been handed down since 1930. First of all, they suspect it's a second-rate prison because it's so full of blacks. In any decent thirties flick the only jigs in the joint were woolly old sheep, full of deep-seated religious problems and enough leftover humanity to make them sound philosophical. Here the young street expatriates might have more savvy, but they aren't that interested in consoling the white man over all his mental hernias. They're just as apt to say: "Man, lay that shit down—it's gettin' too heavy in here. You know?"

Kenny strikes me as a movie derelict at times. A white freckle-faced upstate bandit with short curly hair and a brace of bits behind him, he goes through the prison with a sprightly step, collecting status rewards like a waiter in a high-class joint. In County Jail they threatened him with so much time he tried to hang himself—almost made it. His rap at night is full of the curiosities of prison vernacular.

"Hey, thirty-eight!"

"Yeah, man?"

"Got anything to read?"

"Just short-heist. Like I know you're not interested in short-heist, man."

"Fuck you, I haven't jerked off since this morning—pass it over."

"Okay, but it's shitty short-heist. Like the guy doesn't screw the broad until the third chapter."

"Well, what is he screwing in the first two chapters then?"

"His dog."

"Pass it over anyway—I'm a sucker for dog stories."

"Hey, Kenny—did you ever screw your dog?"

"Shut up, motherfuck. I wouldn't talk about your girl that way."

"Hey, Kenny—"

"Hey, Kenny, hey, Kenny! Who's Kenny, your mother?"

"Nah, that's not his mother—it's his sister."

"How do you know, pussy—you been down around the toilet seat again?"

"Can that stuff. I just got a letter from my sister. She's a very nice person."

"Yeah? How's your mother?"

"Tomorrow. In the yard, Playboy."

"Let's knock off this tough-convict talk. The bell rang ten minutes ago, for Christsake."

"Yeah, and the screw on tonight is a mean one. He tried to bust me last time up for talking in the mess hall."

"Really? You couldn't talk then?"

"You kidding? Once you came out of that cell, buddy, you buttoned up, shut up, and snapped shit. These old motherfucking hacks would like to bring all that back, too."

"Man. I don't think I could've taken that."

"You'd take it after six months in the Box."

"Yeah, I guess you're right."

After-bell chatter is out after eight in Reception. I guess everywhere in the prison. The hacks make their half-hour rounds, and some of them are wearing sneakers. They slither down the gallery like snakes through ruins.

This is a dry basin of the mind, one you hunch over in a frozen delirium and try desperately to puke in. But it's nothing except dry heaves . . .

Eight months in County, waiting and hoping for a break, and now more than a year of this to face.

Time. Is it really made of rubber, does it really stretch? Can I sit here and contract it all, the endless days of this before me, into a sick moment, a shudder in a bad dream? Black outside the windows, pitch. *Whump, whump, whump*—the shotguns. Somebody's trying to imagine somebody's escaping. Maybe they do that every night, with the guns. Shooting at nothing, shooting down into blackness.

Which is greater, the fear of blackness or the fear of whiteness? Can a blind man tell you? No, he can only prophesy, and in his prophecies you will discover whatever it is you fear . . .

I'm afraid of losing my mind.

Completely.

Maybe there's something in the Bible . . .

I can't see spring.

Out in the yard everything looks gray. Gray Spring, your blossoms emiting noxious fumes, like the canisters carried in canvas jackets by the hacks up over the mess hall.

How did the blob of butter get on the ceiling? A good eighty-foot shot, sure to attract attention—must have been the mess help, making bets during cleanup. If I shot a blob of butter up now, what would happen?

Nothing, because I'm back in my cell. But this whole thing, this routine structure, seems at times so fragile anything could break it. The tension is tremendous in that place, but if you pay attention to your food, you can overcome it. The trouble is, my mind keeps wandering. Sometimes I'm not sure I'm here—it all seems very unlikely.

How good it would be to see a few trees.

How good it would be to shoot the breeze. Yard talk goes something like this:

"Motherfuck this place. They didn't even give me pants that fit."

"So take 'em to the tailor shop. The girls will fix you up."

"Yeah. How do you do that?"

"Wait till they assign you. You'll get to know the ropes. You can walk around here in tailored duds, like that dude over there."

"Man, that's a she."

"Kinda cute, ain't she? You see that one staring at me in the mess hall this morning?"

"You mean that little whore? She's been all around the prison."

"So who's looking for virgins. I'm going to get me some of that before long."

"Not me. I ain't messing around. My lawyer says he'll have me out of here in a month or two."

"Who is he—F. Lee Bailey?"

"He's the best criminal lawyer in Rochester, man."

"Seligman?"

"Dig it."

"You're full of shit. Seligman never got nobody sent here."

"I copped a plea."

"Beautiful. Best lawyer in town, and you copped a plea. That makes sense."

"He's fixing up a habe for me. The D.A. didn't keep his promise."

"A habe? You mean a *coram nobis,* don't you?"

"Well, something like that."

"Man, you ought to learn to write your own writs. Those lawyers will screw you every time. See that Indian over there? They really socked it to him. Soon as I get my law books back, I'll have him back in court, you'll see. I sent fourteen guys back last bit—ten of them got a break."

"How's your case coming."

"Shit. Let's take a walk. I can get anybody out of here except myself."

A walk around the yard reveals all the discrepancies and anomalies of prison life. Some of these jerk-off artists couldn't make it on the outside, and that's a fact.

Others never tried. But their stories all seem to have one thing in common, at least the majority of them. An early brush with the law and a lasting taste of bitterness ever since. Some of the predicaments leading to their involvement are heartbreakingly funny. Little boys, playing cops and robbers—but only playing with half a deck.

An alcoholic spree and a fat blank checkbook. A neighbor's cow and a graduate course in sodomy. Dandies and derelicts, dudes and duds. Damn fools who thought they were breaking into the First National but couldn't find the right address. Cowboys who never got west of Canarsie.

Then there are the blacks. They smolder by themselves, more or less. The fat black majority, raising the roof of the mess hall with its voice, its laughter—even in here its laughter—its calls, its signs, its recognitions from four tables over. A steady roar of sound, punctuated by shouts and laughter. They know each other, they laugh at each other, they are all relatives, flesh-deep and freaked out and funky.

A lazy power is in them. They know this prison was built for them—they know they own it. The hard-core groups do not laugh so easy. They sit stone-faced, staring straight ahead or down at their food. Often at no food—they are fasting in the name of Allah. They are the prisoners of the Infidel; they will eat no more than it takes to nourish their hard, lean bodies, vehicles of spirits purifying themselves until they attain a heart with the strength of a hundred men.

Victims.

But the Messenger has thus appointed them to this role. To show the Infidel that his victims are stronger than he. Outside, their yard time is occupied with rigorous group calisthenics, jogging, jawboning, and joining hands in prayers of thanks to the Almighty Allah for offering them this opportunity to serve Him. And, of course, to his Messenger, Elijah Muhammad, for reminding his chosen of the power of blackness . . .

But do they really know it? Do they really know the power of some of these people, their very own brothers, to see and perceive even beyond the limits of their blackness? Without the laughter they are dead men.

Who has the power to laugh in this place has the power of God.

Today is the day. I got a call-out for an interview over at the school, D-Block. That can only mean they plan to assign me there. But I don't want to teach in here. I don't want to do anything in here.

It's not just a matter of cold feet. I'm cold all over. My bones have turned cold. My lower back is a mass of pain at times. This corset sucks—I wore it to the shower even though I thought sure it would make me look like a fag when I stripped. But that business might as well get settled at the outset. The only person who can make you look like a fag is yourself. And you do that by worrying about it. And who gives a fuck. I've got death in one hand, but I don't want to admit it. If I admitted it, somebody might try me—and I don't want that to happen. I just want to get out of here.

These two weeks have seemed like a month.

The longest month of my life. But it's going to be over now. The interview at the school went well. I don't want to go there, but I don't know where to hell else I could go, either. D-Block's supposed to contain the elite.

Imagine that. Imagine how I wept the first time alone in my cell, the first day of Reception. What did it was Herbie, bringing the tomato juice and tobacco. And Willie with the cigarettes. Suddenly I wasn't alone in this place, and I'd been feeling very alone, so I wept.

But I'm not going to write all that crap down. Everybody weeps. You learn to do it silently in here. Out of deference to your fellow inmates, actually. It's bad enough to lose—to have to hear grown men crying stirs only feelings of self-contempt. To make any man feel any more contempt for himself than he already does after the courts have finished with him is contemptible. The mark of a sissy . . .

Over in the school, the head man sits in a little office behind a little desk and does his best to look big. Mr. Big Stuff. Napoleon in glad rags—who do you think you are? With your conservative suit, your silvering temples, your successful insurance-man demeanor, your tie a concession to color in a place of paler shades of gray. You've seen a lot, and you know you must never appear to be weak. Your face gets red when the convicts demonstrate anything close to intelligence. You know your rose garden needs protection, and that's your main job.

Sometimes it gnaws at you that you're dealing with losers every day. But that's your job, and you see to it your record's spotless. Because your next move is an office in Albany, away from places like this, away from problems of people society didn't want. Forget that you've been in them for twenty years. You've been tough, it hasn't cracked you; you can stride through the halls, despite your diminutive stature, hands thrust in pockets (this is another distinction; *prisoners* can't put hands in pockets), your head down, your jaw outthrust, and cut quite a figure while you plan your next speech to the Ladies' Auxiliary on How to Prevent Crime in Your Neighborhood . . .

"We have a tremendous problem here," you start to say—but you don't say it. Because you see that what you're really dealing with is just another loser. A mouse, this guy—he won't cause any trouble. Therefore you can show him your tough side and dispense with preliminary remarks the I-know-this-must-be-tough-on-you-but-Jesus-Christ-with-two-degrees-and-a-family-you-should-have-known-better kind of thing—no need for that at all. This guy looks wiped out. This guy's had it—he's no threat.

"I'm looking for a man," he says, pink-faced, stern,

29

serious, no-bullshit kind of voice; this is a correctional institution, if you aren't a man we'll finish you, "to run a visual-aids education lab. Can you do it?"

I chortle. "Can I do it? Boss, I'se your man, sho 'nuff. If anybody can keep these niggers under control, Boss, it's me."

His face registered mild surprise. His finely chiseled features glowed duskily in the noonday sun. His prognathous jaw drooped just a trifle. The circumflex of his eyebrow formed a Gothic arch as the tip of his cigarette ash fell upon the neat crease of his trouser leg.

He brushed it off with a daintily manicured fingernail. "This is no joking matter," he said seriously. "If you want to be a Boy Scout, you'll have to watch your rutabagas."

I saluted and turned away, farting "The Star-Spangled Banner" as I walked out the door.

I knew for certain I'd gotten the job, thanks once more to *The New York Times*.

Now I lay me down to sleep, I pray the Lord my soul to keep.

The Professor snickers and looks disdainfully at the manuscript. "This isn't something you'd put in a short story," he says. "What purpose does it have in here? Furthermore, it's embarrassing to the reader. The use of italics is an obvious device, a substitute for genuine manipulation of form, technique. I can't say much for this story —you better take it back and think it over. Read James, Colette. Would Lawrence have handled a theme this way? What is your theme, anyway? A son being reunited with his father? But this is all a lot of painful . . . Well, you just better try again."

The past is a bucket of ashes. But the wind blows from all directions, the bucket becomes the center of a vortex, sifting a fine organic deadness throughout the molecular structure of memory, like fertilizer reactivating frozen cells. Such bringing-to-life is pain, is blood spilled on a cheap, worn-out linoleum on a cold night in February, down where the wind blows up across the glazed surface of a river across erect and broken cattails, the winter stalks still poking up through snow.

Mill Street. An aging woman delivers her daughter's child in the middle of the afternoon; the ambulance has taken its time—Mill Street is on the other end of town; there are no emergencies there that can't wait.

Aquarius. A water sign, a swamp, a river. The portents are ambiguous, the odds a fragile balance between life and death. But the mother is healthy and curses the karma of an empty bottle even as she loses her blood. A taxi gets there first, and they both go to the hospital in style.

What does it mean, what is the theme of this story?

Only the professor knows. He has a theory. It can wait. He is not responsible for anyone's mortal soul, anyway. The publication of his book, long awaited among academic circles where poetry is compared to drafts of very old, dry sherry, might get him something at Harvard. Maybe even Oxford or Cambridge . . . *The Forms of Loss*, it's called. All emotions under control, not an embarrassing line anywhere. He'd gone over them with a fine-tooth comb for the last seven years.

And what does this have to do with prison. Whose memory are we invading now, Vietnam-style? Get yourself together, Mother—you've got a long, rough trip . . .

She has red hair—auburn, actually—pale skin, ample breasts, and dark nicotine stains halfway up her fingers. I don't know who she is, I am a little frightened by her visits. She walks in at night, reaches down into the crib, takes my foot in her hand, and raises it to her lips.

It's very embarrassing. I don't know just how to feel about it. I go to sleep and later have nightmares in which I see eyes moving around in the wall.

They tried to bug me out in Reception. They kept me there a week longer than usual, waiting for me to blow. Then it's Observation and Dannemora, maybe Matteawan—one of those dark places away from the sight of God. Once you're labeled psycho, they can do anything to you they want.

"I can do anything I want," she said, the little bitch. I couldn't have loved her more—not then. I can love her more now. Time and distance only increase the feeling. She took acid before I did. But up in Scarsdale, they learn very young. I never even smoked a joint till I was twenty-two. It took me six more years to get high.

"You're too slow," she said up in Boston. Boston is Boy's Town. All the girls go there to meet a man from Harvard. A professor, preferably—old enough to have hang-ups too complicated to show up in bed. She'd been tripping down to the Village since she was fifteen, high on Dex or downs or both, or whatever Daddy had brought home from his office on Fifth Avenue. But you could always get it around the school—everyone had it, everyone was high.

Wanted to write about her first LSD trip. Well, why not? Christ, if they can write about anything, that's something. Most of these girls don't even know where they've been all their lives. Maybe she knows she's been lost. But she's a hard-ass little bitch, knows there's no trouble on earth Daddy won't come and bail her out of.

But why am I thinking these thoughts? Is it me thinking them? I am empty, a dry basin. I am the steel that surrounds me. I am the rivet heads that seal me in, Christ on an Iron Cross—*ack-toom! Jawohl, sehr gut,* officer! Come wake me with your laser beam every half hour, you cocksucker. I never sleep. I am never awake. I don't exist. They have spent all this money on me to confine me, and I don't even exist.

C'est rien. J'ai mal de tête. But I keep thinking of my mother, a stranger in the night. Years of this for her— a state mental institution. And now we know what state institutions are, eh, amigo?

There's justice in this and maybe even some poetry. They let me have my notebooks because they knew they were full of such bad poetry, such whimpering, simpering shit. "This guy's finished," the officer in the Public Safety Building must have said. "Let him have his playthings. He's a Dannemora shot, for sure. Christ, that acid must be bad! You know what? If I ever catch some son of a bitch giving it to my kid, I'll cut his balls off!"

Well, I'll fill these notebooks somehow—De Sade

wrote a novel on toilet paper. I really think prisons have improved since then. Now they don't give a shit what you do as long as you keep your big mouth shut.

God bless you, Mother. They let me keep your letter, too. If I only had a Darvon, I could go to sleep.

You know how it is, Mom. Please don't die till I get out.

The childlike scrawl said everything:

Dear Bill,

I got your lovely letter and was glad to hear from you. It's better to forget the past believe me the present mine at least has its ups and downs. Normally today you don't know how it'll go or what next.

It's cold out today a few days ago it was mild just like spring.

We go to the store and take walks.

Every day I go down to the Maine Store in the afternoon. It's farther away than the one near Edgewoode.

We get out but we never know whether we can as we can't go when the weather's bad. We're thankful when the back door is unlocked.

I just got a package from Phyllis yesterday.

The shoes are a little small but I can wear them. Hope you get out of your difficulties.

All for now.

Love,

Elsie

So it's "We." She was telling me how to do my bit.

Yes, Mother—there are other people in here, aren't there.

We

Who are we?
The prisoners.
What are we doing here?
Waiting.

The guy next door to me is waiting for his parole. A farmboy, strictly upstate. He hardly ever says a word. I don't talk to him, either. Hardly. What is there to say?

39 Company, 40 Cell. Now I'm oriented; now I'm looking out over C-Block, not at Reception—I had my alphabet mixed up before; it was B-Block, the metal-shop people, I was looking at from there. Dark shadows, filing past low arched windows as they march to evening mess.

On my right is the farm kid, worrying about how to write a letter that will give him the job he needs for parole. On my left is another upstate guy, and he's even quieter. Both short-timers. Maybe they were semi-articulate once, but the fear of making a slip this close to the wire has gotten their tongues. It's gotten mine also, and I have at least a year to do in this place.

This place, this place, this place. How many times have I said that in my life: "I want to get out of this place."

More interesting is the guy down in 42 Cell, the last one on the gallery. Very intense, doing his best to hold it in. He's got a shitload of time to do. He runs the school garden—a privilege for us privileged class of inmates, the school instructors. I'd like to talk to him about a garden, but I don't know if my back can take it. I've got to do something to keep my mind off this. I don't like it here, in D-Block. It's probably the best place in the prison, but I don't like it here.

Ralph, his name is. About forty-two, thin, muscular, his face a study in intensity lines. His eyes absolutely wild. I'd like to talk to him, but I don't know how. I don't know what he's in here for. Maybe I'm afraid of him. Yeah, I'm afraid of him, but beyond that fear I'm curious. He sounds intelligent.

Anyway, they made me an instructor up in Cell Study.

Cell Study is a fuck-off scene. We go there every morning between eight and eight thirty—whenever they decide to call us out of the yard.

It's okay. The other instructors give me the silent treatment. I'm supposed to be teaching English, but I can't remember any. What's the difference between a noun and a verb, a subject and a predicate? I used to know. But my mind won't work half the time, and the rest of the time is spent trying to conceal that fact. I don't like this place. Oh, God, I don't like it . . .

I've never felt so alone. It's the presence of other people, all around you, every waking moment, that does it. I can see why Kenny from Syracuse asks to be put in solitary periodically. If this place doesn't bug you, the other inmates will. There are probably more whites here than in the other blocks. Teaching has status. Shit.

The thing is, I feel so lousy physically my mind tends to play tricks on me. I'm wearing the brace every day now—it helps me to walk to the mess hall—but they won't give me a thing for the pain. So. I'm supposed to think the pain is just something I'm imagining. All illnesses are psychosomatic. Death is psychosomatic. But if I complain, if I start writing letters, it will be too bad. The idea is to stay invisible. Not possible, really, but they're still looking for things to write down in their records. Which goes into your jacket, which follows around until Judgment Day. These people are se

God, really. Only they don't believe in Him. Which is why they need churches. Visibility factor.

We get up in the morning on the first or second set of bells. They go off at six thirty, three of them. Then two more at quarter of. If you don't make those, there's a last one on the dot. But a hack will roust you before then. You've got to get dressed, make your bed, sweep your cell. If you don't make that last one, it's probably a bust. Ten days Keeplock, no yard time.

This end of the gallery is quiet, too quiet. I wish somebody would speak to me. Always, I'm on trial. They won't speak to me till they know what I'm doing here, who I am, and what I am. So it's a test.

Fuck the test. Let me die. Sometimes I pray for it. This is all so goddamned fucked up, I don't know who I am or what I'm doing here. If I could explain it to myself, maybe I could explain it to them. In the meantime, they'll just keep waiting till I bug out.

They'd like that.

The only thing that saves me is yard time. Out there, there are at least some people I know.

Not Kenny any more. Kenny got shipped to Auburn; he'll at least be able to see his wife every week. There's another Kenny down the gallery, too—38 Cell. It's the white end of the gallery (did I say that?), maybe they think they're doing me a favor, sticking me here.

But the guys I feel I know are mostly black, and I see them out in the yard. Willie, zero to seven for burglary, forty years old, a bad-ass in County Jail. I hated him there, I love him here. He was chained to me on the way up. He dug where I was at and gave me cigarettes. The whites don't mingle with the blacks much in here, but fuck them. They probably think I'm a cocksucker for playing cards with the niggers. Let them.

Ollie played football for the University. I shouldn't

even put his name down here, I suppose. He asked me to walk the yard with him the other day.

"Mr. Coons—Bill—walk the yard with me, will you?"

I was honored. He's as treacherous as the rest, but there's something I like about Ollie. He was a superstar, but fuck that. To me, he's just a farmboy from Pennsylvania. It's this part of him that he's tried to kill, but it's the only good part. And deep down he knows it.

"Mr. Coons, what do you think about Jesus Christ? Do you think he was a revolutionary?"

"Of course, he was. He put everything on the individual. That's revolutionary, and Authority can't stand it."

"Ummm. I've heard it said that Christ and the devil are the same person."

How do you answer something like that? Ollie reads philosophical books on religion; his father was probably a Baptist. They'd brought him up from the farm on a scholarship, and he was supposed to be the best back since Ernie Davis, maybe better than Jim Brown. But he couldn't keep out of the girls, and they all wanted his black back heaving over them. The white ones and even a few black ones. Maybe quite a few black ones, but the white ones were more ingenious in finding ways to convince him he was a primitive genius.

Which maybe he was, but nobody had helped him find it, least of all his coaches. The head coach only spoke to him through his assistant; his assistant only spoke to him about football, the necessity for rigorous discipline, for following instructions down to the last detail. Meanwhile, he was balling some pretty rich white chicks. It wasn't long before he had his hands on the best dope in Syracuse, and after that it was simply a matter of carrying gym bags full of cash to distant stadiums across the country.

Ollie had good discipline. He never opened the bags

longer than it took to see they were full of cash. Meanwhile he had cars, broads, anything he wanted.

How you gonna keep 'em down on the farm?

"Mr. Coons, I've enjoyed this discussion very much. I'd like to lend you *Good and Evil* by Martin Buber. I've been reading that lately; we could have a discussion sometime . . ."

Maybe Ollie is protecting me. We walked through the ghetto side of the yard with equanimity. But maybe he is also looking for prestige of an intellectual sort. Either way, it doesn't matter. I know he won't be long in Attica, and so does he. Ollie has wires into the governor's office. He'll end up on an honor farm, playing ball, plucking daisies for an early parole. Five years behind the wall at the most . . .

Right, I am jealous. To know someone's future without knowing your own is painful. I'd give my left nut to get out of here. One walk around the yard and you've seen the whole place.

This is how it feels to get off the treadmill and really find oblivion.

Shit, man; you know—fuck it. This is the Age of Aquarius. Whatever creeps out of the woodwork is anybody's business. I'm going to write, and if they bust me, then I'm busted. Meanwhile I'll sandwich these sheets in between the other drivel. I can hardly read my own handwriting anymore—how are they going to?

I saw the parole officer today and asked him if I could have a typewriter. He kicked me upstairs, back to the school.

"You'll have to ask Mr. D. about that. It's really not permitted in the institution. But there's typewriters up there in Cell Study . . ."

Sure there were. And guys being busted for typing out writs on them, too. Never mind that game.

The yard teems with all kinds of conflicting vibrations. You can measure off one psychic area against the next in a matter of a few paces. A quadrangle with a cement walk around it and about eighty yards' worth of playing field in the middle. Not quite a hundred square for something like five hundred inmates to play around in.

Everybody's got his turf, his territory. Tables are staked out; sit down at the wrong one and you're in trouble. So I don't sit unless I'm invited. And I make sure I'm not invited unless I want to sit.

Usually, I do. It's safer than walking around. You might get stuck with some assholes, but at least it's stationary. Moving around you might run into anything.

The trouble with that is, I'm a walker. Pinochle is the only thing that will hold me, and I'm a lousy player, so I have to be fairly buddies with someone for that. It's not like in A-Block, Reception, where nobody cares. Here, who you hang around with has a definite effect on your image. Probably I'm known by some already as a nigger-lover. That's okay. I can really dig it. Eldridge Cleaver may have been full of shit about some things, but he was right about others. Only those who don't understand that the system looks on them as niggers are really niggers. But that can include a lot of territory.

Wade came up today. I saw him in the yard for the first time, although I'd heard he was in Reception. A really decent cat. He and Ollie were soul brothers in County; here they're exploring the situation more independently. They were crime partners and managed not to fuck each other too much. Which is why they don't have to hang all over each other's ass in here to prove they really didn't mean it . . .

Wade is too much! I really wish he didn't plan to catch the next boat to Auburn. He must be the tallest man in the joint, a black basketball import to the same factory as Ollie. They'd gone out and robbed a motel together, so the story went, and somebody had beaten the manager silly with a baseball bat. So he claimed, but neither one of them was the baseball type, and a positive identification couldn't be made. Ollie drew ten to fifteen, Wade a zip-seven. They both felt lucky.

Wade has a deep voice and smokes a pipe because he likes it. In County he'd asked me about tripping. I spent an hour rapping to him about it, and he said when he got out on bail, he was going to try it.

"I don't recommend anyone do anything he doesn't want to," I said. "Some people probably shouldn't—they don't have the imagination to cope with it. Also, the acid in the streets these days sucks. It's not pure; they boost it with shit like speed and strychnine, which is crazy and bound to give you a bad trip sooner or later. Pure acid is hard to find, but it's your mental attitude that counts."

"Well, do you think I could make one without getting all fucked up?"

I laughed. "How long you been here waiting for trial?"

"Eleven months."

"And you're still whipping everybody in chess. Yeah, you wouldn't have much trouble."

"I'm going to do it."

He did. His lawyer beat the first set of charges, and he got out on bail for the second, less serious ones. He'd cop a plea for them later, but in the meantime he wanted to try that trip.

"It was groovy," he said in the yard today. "Man, did I get fucked up! I was crawling all round on the floor, like a dog. Only it was funny—I kept laughing at what I was doing, you know? Like I'd keep remembering I was on a trip, and that would start me in laughing at whatever was going on."

Wade's a man, and it makes me sick to see him in here. This is no place for a man, it's a place for misfits.

Yeah. Here and the United States Congress.

I can't make it on this gallery. The guys won't talk to me, and I'm afraid to open my mouth. I don't give a fuck about their attitudes, and maybe they know it. I don't give a fuck who I walk with in the yard, either. The thing you're supposed to do is start establishing a power base. But I've been through too much . . .

"Mr. Coons, I guess you know— There's something about you. I don't know what it is—"

"You must learn to write a complete sentence."

"I know it. I'm stupid."

"Not stupid—just inexperienced. It takes awhile to know the game."

I didn't say that, of course. The ice was bending the trees low, forming Gothic arches down the driveway. The air was dense, heavy, wet as an overloaded sponge. And cold. Such cold does not occur at Arctic temperatures.

So put another record on and let the fire burn. Lee Konitz, doing "You Go to My Head."

It's a fantasy of the worst sort. If she had a head, she wouldn't be there, bugging you over a subtle nuance of a feeling she had the day before. She wouldn't be banging you in the eyes with all the rich misery of Scarsdale. She wouldn't be pretending she had feelings. Dexedrine had rotted them all out long ago. Now she ordered her rooms painted purple; she lay in them like a pint-sized version of Daisy Miller, dedicated to premature burial of everyone who tried to tell her there was anything in life she couldn't do, anything in the world she couldn't have.

The phone was cradled in the comically plump fingers of her left hand. Her right one was busy prying apart the lips of her jet-set vagina. She was willing to do anything with this man, and he just kept on not really taking her seriously.

"I'm going to make you a slave," she said. "For life."

He didn't even answer that one.

Anger made her blood roar gently, her fingers move faster.

"I'm going to destroy you," she said. "Inch by inch."

"You'll just be tearing up pieces of yourself," he replied.

"I know it," she admitted—rather too quickly, she thought afterward.

"Good-bye, Mr. Coons," she said.

"No. Don't say that."

"Good-bye, Mr. Coons."

"You shouldn't ever say that."

"Why don't you go out and commit suicide? Tonight."

"I've got other things to do."

"Motherfucker."

"They teach you that in Switzerland?"

"Motherfucker."

"Jesus, I hope I can send my kids to boarding school. They'll never learn English over here."

"I hate you."

"I love you."

"I know it."

"Well, look. I'll see you sometime over vacation, okay? I've got to go now."

Such lame shit. And in the bar it was worse. The sound pounds out pneumatically, using the eardrums as slingshots for space launchings.

Only there's no moon. Only the surface of her thighs, white, eerie, unbelievably smooth, electric to the lips.

There's no music for it.

I've *got* to write.

My cock is burning up. Memory can't do this—she must have made a molecular disturbance.

Which is my fault. I wanted to see what would happen because maybe it would turn out to be something great.

It almost was. Five foot what? Jesus, a shrimp—I didn't even notice her legs. I figured she had them, and that was that.

Fool. The first time she called up should have been the tip-off. It was, but I didn't want to be tipped off. Not any more—there'd been too many of these tip-offs in the last few years.

What I wanted from her was to be left alone, and sometime I might give her a thought or two when I was jerking off. Maybe I'd even mention her to my wife if *she* happened to be jerking me off. The chances were, I would have forgotten her in no time flat.

Sooner. But then she came out with this "I've just got to see you," and I knew that when I was really desperate for someone to see, she would be it.

Goddamn her. My throat aches like somebody had a rope around my neck. Is this making her happy? Fuck her, she's probably really gotten married . . .

I can't help it. Jesus Christ, can you hear me, are you listening to these thoughts? Well, then, I want to tell you something: I love her.

Please. Please. Please.

APRIL

Last night the hack caught me writing, so I flushed it. They really don't care, I guess, but everything you do is evidence. Parole hearings are just trials, illegal tribunals. Somebody like me, they'd like to bug out—it would prove all their pet theories and disembarrass them of any more pretense toward human feelings.

Doctor D.'s theory is that a criminal is a social suicide. Like he never heard of a society committing suicide. He's an Episcopalian minister and wears a poker player's smile, but he'd dirk you in a minute. Probably got his degree through a mail-order house. Up in this neck of the woods, the clergy and the cops trade nigger jokes over drinks down at the Legion Hall. Going to work every day here must be like going to the zoo for them. Please don't feed the animals. My mind gets overrevved at times like this, and I have to fight to control it. Writing helps some.

Rumor is now that Fourth of July will be the *day*. D-Day. Dada, by Salvador Dali, using goose grease and human tissue, slapped against cold steel with dried blood as a medium. A few hairs. Really a fantastic artist, but it all gets wiped away with a high-pressure hose.

The lights go out at ten, and there's really not enough glow from the gallery overheads to read or write by. Jerry says he hooked up a mirror in C-Block so a beam would be reflected into his cell. That way, he was able to write up a *coram nobis* and get back into court. He's brilliant—his whole thing will be squashed by the time he gets out. Doing a zip-three, like me. Only I don't have the energy to go into those law books.

Living from day to day is about all I can do right now. Looking at your face in a mirror in this light scares you. I see an old man, his teeth rotting, his hair falling out, his eyes gone blank. Memory trips are like fine little knives, slicing your brain to headcheese.

Sick thoughts. Why put them down, it's a waste of paper. But they won't let me have a typewriter, so it doesn't matter. Faulkner wrote in longhand, which is why it took him hours to say anything. Probably had beautiful handwriting, too—the kind you can't read. Christ, what a wasted-looking man. Bourbon can do that to you, I suppose. Wonder what he would have been like on an acid trip. Probably would have turned into a statue in some little hick-town park, waiting for the cracked bell to toll. Waiting for the *Robber Tee-Lee,* a Chinese junk that plied all the inland waterways but never quite found the sea.

In order to understand rivers, you have to know the sea. Melville did, but his discovery was torturous. How such people ever write at all is beyond me. If you do it for money, you might become rich. Fitzgerald was afraid he might become rich, so he blew it all living the way he thought a millionaire should. That must have annoyed a lot of people. Rich people.

Writers. They all suck. Not one of them ever had anything more to say than my daughter, and she said it all the day she was born.

I can't write about that. I don't care what anybody thinks. If that isn't where it's at, where is it?

Today in the yard I walked around with Jerry. He's something else, an out-of-sight walker. Too bad he's on the other end of the gallery; our discussions never really end. I've drifted away from my original people in here. But Christ, it's good to have somebody to talk to. Up in Cell Study you keep your lip zipped and stare at the moldy lesson sheets, trying to make sense out of them.

At least they moved me out of Elementary English. Teddy has that now. He's a fuck-off artist, a stone-cold killer. Old man's a big deal in the space effort, or he'd be doing nine lives, that cat. As it is, he'll probably get out in eight.

Still, I feel kind of sorry for him. Like you would for a crippled child who doesn't know he's a crippled child. He sucks around the joint like a lame paper boy, trying to remember the secret word that will give him the power to fly. But he ain't going nowhere, nohow, and only everybody else seems to know it.

A tough kid from the suburbs. In and out of court throughout his teens, till the judge got tired of trying to read the truth behind those shifty big brown eyes. Too many boarding schools probably. Too much money to spend and never enough. So you learned to bum, con, and grift. You learned the football ticket thing and a half a dozen other things.

Christ, there were times when you'd suck for a buck. You could live your way across the country for nothing, one beach party after another, everybody's open-air barbecue, steal a radio when you were uptight, shag some pool, stiff a waitress, roll a drunk, mug some fat-ass fag. It was all just a kick, at times. Then it became Big Business, and how the hell did you explain that to a dumb-ass judge?

They were all the same: stupid. They let you off the hook so many times you forgot you were a goddamned fish, nothing but a little fish in a big, big pond.

That's what hurt—the realization of that. Always to be the last in line for the Big Action. So you had to prove that you were just a little bit this side of the line when it came to separating the men from the boys. They saw that coming, too—which is why you got the job of snuffing the motherfucking son of a bitch.

"Even if they found you, nothing would happen," Harold, the pickup man, had said. "Hell, baby, you're the kind of guy that never goes to jail, and you know it."

Sure, he knew it. But even the old man's political connections couldn't beat a murder-one without a cop-out to man-one.

Manslaughter. Well, that's just what he'd done, slaughtered the son of a bitch. The rotten little cocksucker. It had been fun, pumping them into him.

It had been fun watching his face as Nerveless Teddy, the guy who'd never quite go all the way, did it to him. All the way . . .

Cell Study sucks shit. You could say that over and over in your mind, and it still sounded groovy.

"Cell study sucks shit, man," he said to Brownie from C-Mess.

"Yeah, I know, but at least you get to rap," Brownie comes back. "You really think you'll beat this joint by September, huh?"

"Nothing can stop it. I'm making up the writ now for my lawyer to drop in Circuit. He'll push it, too—you wait and see."

"Me, I ain't waiting, baby, and you know it."

"Yeah. You're getting out, you bastard. When's your date?"

"I see the Board the eighteenth. Third time around —they got to send me."

"They'll send you. And my ass'll be sitting right here in this place."

"Yeah. But dig. You said you got connections out there."

"It's beautiful. If you want in, I'll tell you who to talk to."

"Sounds interesting."

Then the voices die down to a low hush, the Doctor takes his stroll through Cell Study, looks disapprovingly at Teddy and his student from C-Mess.

Teddy's blowing, I think, but he doesn't know it.

His friend, a round-faced spade, good nature written all over him, is just indulging. He's on his way out, and he doesn't mind spending half the day like this.

I feel sorry for Teddy.

Everything I never had, and somehow he still manages to remind me of myself . . .

April is the cruelest month . . .

Dead lilacs in the prison dooryard bloom, spilling forth from the mouth of Whitman's corpse, and I never finished writing about Teddy.

Never mind that. What's happening now is what's not happening now. Namely, letters from home.

So, she stops writing, and I know what the next step will be. But I can't face it now, so I'll just let it be. But I've given up writing her. I'm afraid of the nonreplies.

The darkest thoughts never get on paper. Night thoughts or even day thoughts—and those that belong to neither category. The shit I wrote in County Jail is lousy; I ought to flush it. Who needs such proof of existence? That's all beside the point now. I've got to do something about my back or I'll go crazy.

The reason jailhouse poetry is generally so bad, Wilde included, is that it attempts to give legitimacy to feelings we are still in the process of trying to cope with. Poe's poetry is prison poetry in that sense. He had all the emotional apparatus of a clever high-school girl. His moods have little variation. Only his images stand out as something worth considering. He could build them, step by step, until they became larger than the poem, until they consumed everything the poem had started out to be. The fascination of horror is in the eating, eating . . .

If you don't eat everything on your tray, you'll be subject to disciplinary action. Some hacks are gentle about it, others not so gentle. Some of them act downright embarrassed by the whole thing, which only makes them meaner to deal with.

So I don't deal with them. To me, they are just props in a Depression film. Once in a while one looks pretty hip, comes in to work with sideburns, but then you don't see him very long. "Up on the wall, mister—you can wear your hair any way you want, but we don't have to look at it during mess!"—the Captain.

I'd feel sorry for some of these hacks, but such feelings are outlandish in this place. The main rule is not to feel sorry for anybody—and first of all, yourself.

That means not thinking about yourself a great deal. But the routine forces it on you, in a way. This is nothing but organized boredom, disguised idleness, enforced lassitude. I could sleep fifteen hours a day if they didn't have me going in and out of my cell all the time.

The march to the mess hall seems to take hours; we eat in B-Mess five times a week, and it's a long winding walk through the maze of tunnels, a trip that takes your mind clear out of this world at times. It's just painful to look at these bricks; they remind you of nothing except boredom, boredom, boredom. And then all the exquisite little tensions of this place gather themselves together as you approach the dining-room door, only to burst in a roar of discordant cacophony as the hack motions you across the threshold.

Eating becomes a game of guessing what the food might have tasted like before they cauterized your taste buds. Even the food tastes like boredom. But that's a mercy becauuse the odor suggests something else again.

But it's not that bad. So far I haven't seen a single maggot. Eating is a human conceit, anyway. We don't quite fall under that category anymore.

Love. I was going to write about that. There's so much to say about it, and I don't know where to begin.

With my wife? God bless her. Part of me wants to hate her, but I won't let it. If I looked at her actions apart from anything else, I couldn't stop it. But I know what she's into, even if she doesn't quite understand all of it herself. Conditions of survival in the Land of Plenty require sometimes the most painful and scrupulous kinds of sacrifice. It says so in the Old Testament, the only reliable account of what's happening. It all happened before. It will all happen again . . .

The crucifixion. The bloody fight for a front-row seat. The circus stands full of doctors, lawyers, clergymen, cost accountants, pimps, fags, foreign-film actresses, and other freaks. The mob howling for more, more, more . . .

Anything to take our minds away from a single day in this hellhole of existence. In the theater of the absurd there are no heroes, only amiable fall guys. The bailiff wears a knowing smile. They think because they're out on bail they're free. The state loves nothing better than bail-jumpers. All that grease keeps the Big Wheel turning, the atomic-powered torture rack, or How to Make Money Exploiting Human Hang-Ups.

In the meantime I am thinking of her. Not her, but *her*—the real Her I don't want ever to think about again, because the vibes laid down by such feverish cerebration are bound to melt these metal cages and cause some jackass to start shooting. I bet I could hit that rivet overhead, the shiny one with the smiling face and sloe brown eyes that make my fucking heart pump faster, and this is madness in here.

The cold creeps into your bones and sucks the marrow from them. They use it for soup at evening mess. It keeps the cannibals happy, it makes them content. The Witch Doctor down the gallery gave me the eyeball tonight. He's just part of a clan what's out to murder all whites in time of emergency. Like when they cut down on the rations, you dig? I gave him my best smile, the one that says: "You're cute, too, but I'm still thinking of a good piece of ass."

Maybe someday she will be. Hell, she is now, I know it, that's what hurts. She turned her boobs in profile for the camera, knowing I'd eventually get to dig the shot. I did in County Jail and it hurt. I didn't want to go to prison anymore, no, not really . . .

So I pasted her up against the wall and imagined what they'd look like by the time I got out.

Fantastic, and she still wouldn't be old enough in the eyes of the law. But then, nobody is . . .

Frantic. Who the shit would have thought of this— except me? The product of all my paranoia freak-outs put together. The biggest put-on since the Electric Chair, a group that died of anemia during a West Coast Brown-In. Christ, what a trip!

But there's more to it, this can't be the end, this can't be the time, this can't be the place . . .

MAY

I'm going to make sense of this someday. I'm going to figure the whole thing out and sell the story to *The New York Times*. They really need me. I'm vital to the malfunction of any internal disorganism. I'm sick, and that's a fucking fact. This isn't a cold I've got, it's slow creeping death. All the doctor can do is encourage it along by refusing any serious medication.

"Five days cell time," he says knowingly. Cases like this can continue for years, but you never know. If he passes out in the hall, we might give him a shot at the hospital. But this is a prison, and you're supposed to suffer. Fuck him and his cold.

So fever raises high the hopes of eventual delirium. Death might be sweet, but let me go easy. I have tasted of thy fruit but sparingly, O Lord; let not my lips be sealed by hopeless terrors, nameless as my crimes may be. In the name of Jesus Christ, amen.

You can see it, mental dada dangling before the mind's eye. But it's nothing—only cold steel that won't get out of your face, ever.

Meanwhile, memory. Mary sitting on the back-door stoop, stoned by the sight of Sunday morning mites scurrying furiously in the dust. Blond, blue-eyed, a cornflower girl, fragile, at peace, distant, immediate, real. A lady already at three.

"Daddy," she says, "Daddy—once *I* was a bug."

Her eyes turn up to me, mystic seas of blue. Am I mistaking what she said? The bugs are crawling around in a perfect frenzy.

"Once I was a bug," she repeats. "And we were running, and we said: 'Look out for the Giant Clam!' "

She was perfectly serious; I knew right then reincarnation was true—my children never lied to me.

She was teaching me the law of karma. Related to the flower and mite, toad and meadowlark, hers had been a beautiful cycle of existence. Gentle always, beyond the fear of death or violence, happy to be born, happy to die, she had progressed rapidly to this state of perfection. For this reason I can bear the separation. Joyce, too, is gentle, but her moods run deeper. Earth-red, the color of her hair when she was born. We understood each other completely. I felt her as a spiritual presence, a slender but substantial link to God. We try to forget God, but it never works. We can only forget ourselves. Religion is the only practical truth, but once you organize it, it becomes a prison. In the chapel last Sunday I prayed for my children and their mother.

Who, like mine, I never really knew . . .

Oh, shit.

I can see my sister writing it over and over now, eyes red with angry tears: "Shit, shit, shit, shit, shit!" But she won't send the letter, it's just her way of getting back at life.

Five days. There's nothing to do but write, and I'm almost enjoying it at times, though—or maybe because —my head's still dizzy from this cold. At times I feel almost lucid.

The guys on the gallery take me for a sad sack. Which is just as well; as long as you keep your mouth shut they won't fuck with you—only the out-and-out sadists. And most of those are very insecure when it comes to looking anyone in the eye. Which leaves only the outright maniacs, and they're no more of a danger in here than they are in the streets. Lunatics abound, but in prison you learn to keep a cap on it.

Diz came to Cell Study today and drew the desk in back of mine. One look at his eyes and I know what I'm in for. A long hard hassle to see who's really going to run the place. He'll think he's winning and hate me when he finds out I never really cared that much.

Who wants to run a prison? Any part of one? The job might have its advantages if you can keep your wife under control. That's what all wardens must think at some time. Now, evidently, he's given up thinking. He's made himself into a machine, the kind that hands out cards and letters and reads five-minute speeches from notepaper. . . .

Must keep writing. This is all disjointed, but the worst shit goes down the drain. Ralph the Gardener's toilet was stopped up last night, and I thought he'd freak out. Umpteen years to do and almost that many behind him and he's still a nervous wreck. For that I have to admire him somewhat. His hatred is naked, near the surface—and just barely under control. Jerry says he's violent, someone to look out for. But I could relate to him, except for the big time difference. Anybody with less than ten in this place is supposed to be a weak sister. Jesus, what a guy! He has education, reads heavy shit. But he won't speak to me and I won't speak to him.

That's the only way to get along on this gallery, it seems, at least if you're white. The blacks rap at night, but there's little real leisure in it, like at County Jail. But there was also hope there—abundant hope that some-how things would work out. After the militants dug I wasn't trying to be on their side, we had some good raps. I stopped leaving my cell with that vague fear that some-body might kick my head in the moment I turned my back. Ollie told me football stories even a sportswriter couldn't invent. Even the Mau Maus began to eye me enviously. It got to be one big party, pitch and gin and pinochle, only I stayed out of the bridge because the arguments in that tight circle often bordered on real violence.

You had to dig it, though—those guys really loved each other. Wade was the most beautiful cat of all—always in the middle of it, always controlling it at the right moment with his deep, sonorously masculine voice. After a while, some of the black berets began to disappear.

In some ways I actually wish I were back in County Jail.

No, not really.

Just out of here, out of *here*.

Sometimes the desolation of her nether regions left me sweetly sad. Was this all she had to offer the world? Even so, it was a great prize, worthy of all the crusades.

She was Catholic ass at its finest. A willingness to do anything so long as she could talk about it at some later time. All Catholics are potential writers.

The desolation of her asshole. Bleak and barren in the noonday sun, shaded by mangroves. Why the asshole? All of her was perfect; nothing was wanting wherever you looked. Why plunge it in, then, in this tiny aperture, the least dignified entrance to the holy temple of her body?

It wasn't a conventional asshole. Whatever you might say about such things, she herself was the inspiration for the most depraved speculations imaginable. Anyone would know she'd never be really opened up by a straight fuck. Anyone who studied such things.

To be near her any length of time was to turn yourself into just such a student. She was all body; she had never thought of herself any other way, from the first. Her childhood sleep was sensual, orgiastic. Her brown eyes were filled with the knowledge of how it feels to be born. She forgot nothing—consequently she had to feign forgetfulness of everything. She was an only child in a family of five, where it is easy to be ignored, to be an only child.

To love her was at first a subtle form of madness. She provoked it with every motion—but so innocently, you'd go through hell trying to explain it to yourself.

Afterward. After the soft curve of her correctly cushioned ass had made itself known to you in ways not even a thoughtless child could devise. After she had said things to you a true woman in heat would strive to think of— matter of factly, like afterthoughts.

Lolita was full of shit. A fucking intellectual masturbation. Humbert never knew what America really felt like. He never held it to his crotch and said to hell with everything else. He never bled for it while fighting for self-control. He never cried because to cry over her was a blessing granted only to those who were willing to be destroyed. He never loved her because he was afraid of getting really lost in her eyes.

The Great Fear—getting lost in spaces so vast as to make time a completely different dimension. Not even in Russia could you encounter so much in so small a place. To journey up her thighs with your fingertips was to feel the curve of the Milky Way. To kiss them was to taste the sweet, sweet centers of foreign stars.

"You can do anything with me you want," she said. So sincerely the challenge slayed you, making life on earth insane.

"I believe in God, don't you?" she said another time. The others always asked you first.

"When will I be big enough for you?"

But the cheapest thrills you could get became stellar moments of experience, of communication with something beyond any mortal convention. You could only love her as though she were a woman and hope to God she might become one . . .

This is freaking me out. Imagination, desist!

JUNE

Today should be a great day. It's raining, we won't go to the yard, but somehow I feel something great is going to happen.

Maybe a letter from home. Jesus, that would be too much. But she hasn't written in so long, and I can feel that she wants to communicate with me.

All right, I'll go mad like this. Maybe I'll even jerk off later, when the lights go off. Maybe I'll love my prick with my hand and pretend it's her.

Maybe I'll write a song.

They took her picture away. Or else I left it on the wall in County Jail: I can't remember which.

So when the parole hearing comes up, they might flash the photo; they might even come up with testimony.

"Mister ——, do you remember this picture?"

"Well, I—"

"Just yes or no answers, please—that's all we're interested in."

To consciously lie is to tell them all they want to know.

"Yes," I say.

The gray-haired one nods. "And isn't it true that while in County Jail you—were very attached to this particular photograph?"

"Well, yessir."

"Aha. *Then why did you leave it behind?*"

The criminal always wants to indict himself, is their theory. He will go to great lengths to leave some clue, some trace of his inner personality. I know now I am sunk. Should I freak out? Should I start slobbering like an acid-head maniac?

No, they're half expecting that.

"A guy offered me a pack of cigarettes for it," I lie.

That stops them. I have managed to strike the deepest chords of guilt about the whole Free Enterprise system. What can they be now except sympathetic?

Jesus, let me wake up from this dream, even in a cold sweat.

Perhaps I shouldn't read the last entry; it affects how I write the next.

It doesn't matter. I've always hated the idea of writing a diary, anyway. It's like something you're supposed to do if you're a writer. It's expected.

This is not a diary, this is *New Notes from an Old Underground.* Say you heard it on the grapevine . . .

Clever, you son of a bitch. But why don't you come right out and say what's really on your mind? Is it because you don't know? Or are you simply afraid of new charges, knowing now that a plea of guilty simply means your whole life is on trial? And you are defendant, prosecutor, judge, and jury—what kind of a break would you give yourself?

Six months in a Swedish Funny-Farm, your Honor!

But that's not enough, by Our standards—and besides, the taxpayers can't afford such self-indulgent nonsense.

"For your own good, I sentence you to a minimum of one and a maximum of three years in Attica State Prison —you will be able to receive weekly therapeutic treatment there," he adds in explanation. "Your crime is a bad one."

That's the way it really happened. But the papers when I got here had been changed to read 0-3, a zip-three, which is a different kind of sentence, really the only legal one he could give me, I found out later. My lawyer told me I'd be out of this joint in a few months, but he was a corporate lawyer and I wasn't a corporation.

But why talk about him? Why write all this down, as

though someone were eventually going to read it. Why not just write a good sex scene and jerk off afterward?

But I'm not going to write that one in here.

Or maybe I will and then flush it. The motherfuckers wouldn't let me have a typewriter, after all. Which means they'll have to support me and my family this whole bit. I just pray they don't build welfare ovens before I get out . . .

Jesus Christ, I really pray for that.

Amen.

Nice going, Judge!

"Your crime is a bad one!"

Whom have I murdered? Whom have I stolen from? Whose property have I destroyed?

You think I was destroying your mind, but that is only what you have been doing to yourself, Judge. Let the record be straight on that; let the truth go down—as it never goes down in your cleverly constructed hearings, every illegal tribunal I will be subject to from now till Kingdom Come.

I'm not afraid of that last trial, Judge—are you? I have no trouble sleeping nights, Judge—do you? How are you going to avoid the eyes of my children, even though yours are closed? They will shine brighter into yours, more penetrating than all the flashlight beams of your hired flunkies the world over. They have truth in them, and you can't stamp it out.

There is another record, Judge—one you can't get your hands on; one your hired flunkies can't manipulate and tamper with and bend to reflect the bogus wisdom of all your merciless acts, the products of your willful ignorance.

That record is written in the human heart. Your scarlet letters have become meaningless in that record—your brands, your numbers, your statistics, your endless convenient categorizations, your verbal mousetraps, your dainty fingers curled around your morning cup of tea.

The indictment grows. Who will bear the crushing burden of the weight of history most directly—those who have failed or those who never tried? Those who hardly had a choice or those who sit on gilded thrones of opportunity every day, ignoring the hourglass, constructing subtle prisons of the self?

These secrets you would hide will burst forth one day, just as surely as the earth trembles in its season. Will there be a safe place to stand then?

How many bodies lie buried in the sealed chambers of your mind? I am just a sinner, Judge, but you have attempted to play God. Who will have to pay the greater price?

I don't know, Judge. I can't judge you, Judge. But something tells me you will have to ask yourself these questions, or as surely as the tide before you swells, you will be swept away. Because the perfect society you think you are protecting never existed; it was just an idea in your mind, carefully nurtured in the face of all the facts, fabulously constructed as a means of keeping back the tide.

And this is why you are pitiful and not to be hated. The King of ancient Persia, with a million slaves at his command, couldn't succeed in beating into submission the waves of the ocean he wished to cross. See him now, standing there, blood bulging in his veins, throat hoarse with curses, commands, imprecations, as his legions flail with disciplined futility against the oncoming surf and foam, mixing their sweat with the salt of the sea.

But all this is inane horseshit.

There isn't any judge.

There is only the Mechanism, the Process. At first a system of wheels and pulleys, crude but effective. Later, steam was used, the hard slow fires of the earth made to serve; rivers were subverted, dams built, waterfalls trained to produce a steady voltage. The trouble is, you can't trust men with this much power. So we had to invent more machines—machines that looked like men, that would fool even the closest observer.

But the closest observer was a child who wasn't even there. Her eyes had barely opened when she saw it. The whole thing came to her as a dream, descending from another world.

He was beautiful. His eyes held the world in their centers, and he made me see that I should take my place in it. He told me there were many sorrows in this, but there were also many compensations. But I would have to learn to recognize them, for out of all things that he had to give, I had chosen consciousness.

May God forgive me. To make such choices is to accept the trial of choosing. Which meant that you would be on trial constantly and still must not fear making the wrong choice. He told me that to do this I must be strong as Hercules, I must start kicking out immediately. I must not wait for the Hand That Gives Life, but I must always be ready to accept its blow. He said I was beautiful because I was created in His image. But to know his image I must light my fire all day and read his works till I was blind.

I said: "Father, I'm not strong enough."

He said: "Son, you got no choice. Be strong."

And then he went away. All I seemed to feel after that turned out to be weakness.

And yet I felt strong. I felt that I could take it all and maybe even give some. But I knew that to be caught in such an act would be to find myself branded among men.

FELON.

It's nothing. It's only the love, crying out. It's only the way I see things now—sad, distorted, twisted up like the last used leaves of summer; folded and put away like a paper napkin in a cheap café.

There's no such thing as self-pity. There's only the sorrow of having missed the train of last night's lost existence and waking up to see a light which told you you had now become a substitute in a game whose rules were beyond anyone's ken.

It had never seemed simple. Not while you were playing—but in the breaks there was often tranquillity and maybe even the kind of ecstasy that comes from having played. In the beginning the coach is absent, and you begin to think the game can serve your own little purposes. That's nice—like sunny days before the end of summer. Like girls whose tennis outfits fit them all too well. Like autumn leaves scratching the path of the wind across a dry macadam court the day after the nets are down. Like standing alone in the bleachers and watching her golden hair and thighs, dreaming your night life away.

There are bars and bars in Manhattan. Bar capital of the world, it attracts every man who really needs a home. It couldn't keep me there forever, but it used up some very good years . . .

Jesus Christ, am I really writing this? It seems good to me, but I'm doing it because there's nothing else to do . . .

I can't stand the sight of dates. Any reminder of time is an agony. You might go blot, they might wipe you out, that's the fear. It's the meaninglessness of it that makes it so fearful. This is a moron factory, attempting to produce exact replicas of nothingness.

The Master Moron sits up front, drooling inconspicuously into his Dixie cup. He wears a white shirt, tie, and has lately given in to plaid slacks, form-fit over his softly rounded masculine-feminine figure. Years of this kind of work have not made him soft, so he tells himself in the mirror, they've only rounded off some of the edges. What we have here is really a smooth item—sort of like the nose of a dum-dum. Educated, intelligent, too. And very sanitary, like a surgical napkin.

He toys briefly with the pages of the dossier, examines a manicured fingertip, farts. It's an odorless, noiseless type fart, good for Cocktail Parties, Board Hearings, and even now and then an Inmate Interview.

"What about your love life?"

"It was completely innocent. I never took a virgin under five."

"The record shows you have a sex problem."

"Yes, but I'm sure it will be cured in here."

"Ahem."

"Excuse me—what was that?"

"I said 'Ahem.' You better get used to official jargon around here."

"Yessir."

"That will be all for now. Remember to pray in the name of Jesus Christ."

A real hip parole officer. I would have kissed his ass, except it was so delicate I didn't want to disturb whatever equilibrium kept it from falling out of his pants. But I would say a special prayer for him in Sunday Mass.

The trouble was, I wasn't a Catholic. Catholics can do their bits and charge it off to a minor deviation on the road to eternity. Like a back-country bad trip. Niggerology wouldn't even help you figure out the road signs.

Nevertheless, I consulted the oracle, Mr. G. He lived in the cell next to me, and the only reason I write of him in past tense is that I know he'll never see the light of unwalled day.

Not his fault. All he did was help gang-rape a white secretary-chick who'd been dreaming so hard of it her vibes caught up a lot of Harlem small-fish. He was sorry afterward, too. In those days you could commit a rape without undue bloodshed.

He replaced the salt farmer in the cell on my left. And if he was slightly prone to occasional outbreaks of ultra-rightism, who should be surprised?

I am not. Except he seems to depict me as the wolf, the destroyer of sacred icons, the ultra-left secret underground militant, Captain America in reverse, wielding a left-handed monkey wrench in order to jam up the works. Nothing more conservative than an old con, nothing more wedded to the system.

His story would be touching, except that they're all down on dopesters at the moment. Not so much dopesters as *acid* heads. They don't like acid; they're convinced it's some kind of whitey conspiracy to steal away their source of power, which is a benighted vision of taking their place at the helm of the latest atomic submarine.

But, *mira*, all this is mere spite. I am flipped out and I know it. The vibes in this place are deadly, internecine. It is a monument to the ongoing calamity that is modern civilization.

But I am the ongoing calamity that is modern civilization. These rivets go through my flesh, my sinews, my bones, my brain. This clang of steel against steel, this slaveman shuffle down dark musty corridors—it is me, it is me!

Truly I am going insane. What is there to do, then, except watch and wait—just as it says in the Bible.

I cling to its words for reason, which is perhaps an insane act. Ollie left it to me in County Jail, and now it is full of markings—the diary of an oppressed people, the revolutionary solution proposed by none other than Jesus Christ, whose sacrifice reached to the very limits of consciousness. He bled for the Universal Mind, that it should become known to man. Once on that road, you can stop at nothing; to reverse such a course means damnation beyond belief. So we let consciousness be tortured. We record it, we don't try to stop it—we neither love nor hate it; we do not transplant the warts onto our soul, we let them grow there, the evil spots of our civilization, for the world to see.

In the mess hall you see the one-eyed, the disfigured, the scarred, the wounded, the stuttering, the mute, the testimony of what we have done, what we are, what we are likely to be.

Monstrosities.

Dr. Frankenstein sits in his office, no longer prepared to wander out among his creations. He has three telephones, one a hot-line to the National Guard. He frets. This wall is not tall enough, strong enough—they promised to reinforce it. But where are the allocations? Trim the budget, they say; get things down to the bone. But if we cut rations down much more, these monsters will run amok. If only they could be used for target practice or something . . .

Jesus Christ, what a way to end up—Chief Caretaker in a Monster Factory. Sodomists, mammy-rammers, baby-rapers, motherfuckers—and now they are sending in the worst trash of all: the dynamite crews, dopesters, and middleclass dropouts! How can you run a respectable prison? But one of these days they'd be sending the judges up, too; that was something to think about. Maybe this was a Key Position after all . . .

No. Not to think such thoughts. Subversive thoughts, and the wires of your mind might be tapped. Christ, they'd done a job on the poor slob of a warden at Auburn —really wasted him. Now the commissioner was changing heads, too. Who knew who'd be next? Got to watch it, got to play it cool. One more year here and then a desk in Albany . . .

Hoping some poor bastard would drop dead soon, leaving that much of a vacancy . . .

Hoping . . .

You can't help it. To eliminate on paper is the only escape. The only way. To build a paper tunnel under these walls, to find temporary respite in the wayward reflections of an addled consciousness.

To cope with this *hate*. It is no good; it is impotence given a semblance of life; it is death, scorched, burning, carbonized—still glowing.

So Christ suffered, casting himself upon the wheel of history. In the meantime the Inquisition goes on. I was wearied of it all long before I came in here. Watching all the signs of the times, I came to the conclusion it couldn't go past the year 1969. Some vast sacrifice was needed, one nobody seemed able to provide. Just the regular tired old rituals, a daily bath in blood. But that's all encouraged, just part of the game. They do it to each other daily at the top; if you're at the bottom, look out for the steamroller.

Today I went to church. It's all part of the game, too; they keep tally down front, take a regular Sunday church count—the Parole Board wants to know all about that.

But the idea is to do something. To participate in all this madness and somehow survive it, to make yourself just a little bit more than the madness.

Though you are surely mad. Vanity alone could make anyone think otherwise.

So I went to church and hoped for some contact, some revelation, some indication of something beyond the pain of this existence. The weariness of even the pain. And the pain of the weariness.

As school staff we are allowed to have white shirts. Donny, the company water boy, comes wheeling down the gallery, taking church count: "Protestant services!" he calls out, and in the next breath, "Razor blades!" There's a lineup for that, too, and don't get confused between the two. The razor blades are for shaving, the services are for salvation.

So, white shirt—but no tie; I'm not going that far. I do want to think, I do want to pray—this concession to organized salvation is a two-edged sword, or maybe just a double-edged razor blade, who knows.

Charlie the big black pimp a few doors down goes every Sunday, and I'm glad of that. He's a mean mother from Chicago, arrested on dope and various charges, with a beautiful smile, whose eyes go slightly crazy at times, usually when he is thinking about his time. Wants to be the bull of the gallery, but doesn't have the confidence it's worth it—which is a sign of intelligence.

The curious thing is, he's a *believer*. And I can just see him in some smart black-belt cocktail lounge, the foxes sucking up to him and buying him scotch after a bad day at the races. He'll make it all up that night, but right now it's good to know a few of them still love you just for kicks—afternoon chicks who give it away before nightfall and hustle the rest if you serve them the right kind of dinner. Never had a regular string, but all of the free-lancers came easy. And that was the only way to beat the mob . . .

"Protestant services!" the hack calls out from behind the lockbox at the end of the gallery and pops the cells on his list. I fall in behind Charlie, and thirty-some curious or disinterested pairs of eyes watch us pass in review.

"Do you want to be saved?" Donny chants sarcastically, his farm boy grin taking the edges off it.

I somehow dig Charlie, though we don't rap much, even though he occasionally likes to throw his weight. Somewhere close to two hundred, the only guy bigger being Big Mack, a fiftyish Irishman with graying hair, Instructor in Mathematics, who looms like a great White Whale wherever he goes. But he's a Catholic and simply sneers at us as we pass—a friendly sneer if there ever was one. Mack has more time in and out of joints than most guys on the gallery have years. Nobody fucks with him except Charlie, and they try to keep it grinning. But grinning it up is sometimes very hard to do. Racial tension on the gallery has peaks and eddies. At least the real militants are on the far end. Maybe so the hacks can watch them better—who knows?

I am genuinely interested in Jesus. Why? Because he has survived despite a severely tarnished reputation. And those who tarnish it most, most often stand on the preacher's platform. Their work of justifying man to God goes on unceasingly, despite all the evidence of His indifference to their schemes. And they are His instruments, too —despite all their indifference to Him.

God is a mackerel, made holy by some power-hungry priest. He used it to flail the masses into submission, to which they are led willingly by their ignorance anyway, but no institution can exist without doing institutional violence.

This institution is violence embodied, nurtured, encouraged. The final separation of man from nature—his own nature. But perhaps it is also God's handiwork. If so, I want to see that—I want to see how that could be. I want to see how much this hireling wearing cloth can offend me with his confusion of God with Society before I am done with all his fantasies and lock my door and let them send me to the Box.

HBZ. Housing Block Z, as they call Solitary here. They throw you in a cell and let you rot. You are no longer fit to walk among the prison population. There's a certain status to be gained in having gone there. And few are as conscious of status as a convict. But I'm not in for those kinds of ego trips. I never got up on a stage and told people they should take acid, it cures everything, even history. Maybe Dr. Leary had a point, but I'll never be convinced he wouldn't have traded it all for a reserved seat at the Harvard Club.

The auditorium, which also serves as the chapel, is huge, high-ceilinged, the proper setting for a thirties Nazi indoctrination film. It's gray, but there are flowers on the stage, and if Jesus can make a breakthrough here, you know he's really in. The organ player is something else, a gray-haired cutie from the hospital who shot and stabbed his lover. He plays his instrument like a slow, sad jerk-off to the end of time. But even Tschaikovsky couldn't have helped this scene much. The auditorium fills to about a third, mostly dark faces, many of them here to pass each other love notes in the john.

The preacher looks as old as the mummy of Tut-ankhamen. A corn-country face, complete with skinny neck and bobbing Adam's apple, his rimless lenses casting off gleams of dubious interpretation as he strains his face Lord-ward under the arc lights. He wears a black pin-stripe and reminds you of somebody's funeral. Maybe yours.

Then the service begins. "Keep Silent," the chorus starts singing, and you wish they would. But you can't have everything, Christ knows . . .

Charlie, sitting next to me, is devout; I can see that. His head bends at the right times, and he knows when to say "Amen, brother." His sincerity shames me into deeper reflections on the Meaning of All This, but I can't quite force myself to pay attention to the chaplain; his words drift in and out of my ears like stray flies through a ploughed-under wasteland.

It seems beyond reason that I should be here, wit-nessing this. Was I really one of the Lost Children of the Universe? If so, how had they found me? Whose agents were these, who had forced me to this taste of the bitter milk of human forgetfulness? All around me I heard voices, whispering. I was alone, completely isolated in my thoughts.

This might become a dream and the dream have no end. But then, whose dream? Only the most tired, ungodlike of imaginations could have erected these structures, monuments to hopelessness and futility.

I regretted having come to church, but the thought of Christ imprisoned has its seductions. If it is true that he is in me, now, at this very moment, if the Holy Spirit is never denied to anyone in need, if the Kingdom of Heaven is available to anyone, if the Light shines even into the darkest recesses of the human heart, if to err is human and to forgive divine, then I have not much hope in the hands of those who have all but forgotten how it is to be human. Then I must put my trust in agencies that operate beyond the range of human tampering.

But everything in my life seems to have pointed to this. Which is why, perhaps, I atttempted to abandon reason at the first real opportunity.

To live in the senses, to receive their blessing or their curse. Consciousness is torture—everyone who continues to think sees that in time. But not everyone goes to prison to discover that fact inside its most intimate aspects.

The wearying effect of hypercerebration is well known to anyone who has ever suffered a nervous breakdown. Which is why we have drugs and why so many people take them. It's as simple as that. Our thoughts are stimulated by adversity, but adversity offers no stimulation in return. It merely aids in the process of using up our nervous system. We consume ourselves this way, and it has been made into an economically feasible undertaking. Drugs may help retard the process, but only at a proportional expense to the pocketbook; hence drugs will continue to loom ever larger as an economic factor, an indicator of the poverty of our existence.

Now this idiot-scholar claims in his book that Christ was nothing but a combination charlatan-fakir and weirdo-drug addict. Which, even if true, misses the whole point. He went All the Way, and how many others *really* would go that far? Consciousness pushed to its farthest point, to the utmost limit, absorbing everything, leaving no secrets left to be learned from the human heart.

And beyond that—what? The greatest secret of all —the human heart itself?

Perhaps a universe can be created that operates independently of God's will. Perhaps we will succeed in creating one. Perhaps it will in some way resemble the one we know now. But what does the one we know now resemble, so much as our indescribable ignorance?

May God have mercy!

This is the kind of place you could write about, but it would take a genius, and even he might have to search for words to do it complete justice.

Complete justice is never available, anyway. No crying over spilled milk; all you've got to do is live out a year or so of your life this way. And Cell Study is comparative heaven from what I can see of the rest. Downstairs, they try to cope with the actual problem: getting men on the right road to the Future through reading. Most of them manage with the short-heist somehow. Maybe they just look for the key words. Some of the books passed around don't have pictures. The ones that do are pretty badly thumbed over.

They ought to allow more pornography in here. It would reduce the tension, lessen odds on the Riot. Every prison has to have a riot sooner or later, but I'd just as soon not be around to see this one. It's going to be on grounds that cut deeper than any previous inmate disturbance. The blacks really want to take over this prison, if for no other reason than to say they've taken something over. The line between normal oppression and racism is a thin one—the administration bends over backward sometimes but always manages to land on its head.

Outside agitators, they claim. But there's no such thing. Once you're in here, you're in—the cops can't arrest only model prisoners; the Parole Office evidently, from the figures and the stories, works overtime to recycle men who've already been prison-trained. Today we got a dude who crossed the county line in the car of a friend who turned out to be a setup man for the Parole Office.

He'd do another year in the joint; meanwhile he was going around trying to find somebody who might understand the complexities of his case enough to help him compose a writ. A difficult project—he speaks very little English.

Cell Study is run by the Right Reverend Dr. D., a soft-spoken man with a purse-lipped smile and a gimlet eye. My first impression was he was probably the best man to work under in the institution. But don't cross him. He sees all and has a very strict Episcopalian view of things. A correctional officer of the cloth. If there is a contradiction there, he's worked his way around it years ago.

I have no intention of crossing him. I'm too damn sick to fight, anyway. Each day is an effort to stay awake, to focus the mind on what I'm doing. The envelopes come in from the cellblocks with the lessons scrawled on them in some fashion or other, and at times they might as well be hieroglyphics from the tomb of some unknown civilization.

Being dead, a nonperson, has its advantages. Sometimes this prison shrinks in dimension, becomes a very little place indeed. With the coming of spring the gardens are planted—a privilege given to us because we are deemed trustworthy by the authorities, and I really can't imagine anyone doing a hack in with a spade or a pickax. Not even Ralph, the Mad Gardener.

He's something else. All that lavish emotional apparatus going to waste. It's a tragedy, but what can you do? Tragedy is commonplace in here, where everything is reduced to a level of trivia even Joyce would be hard put to elevate. He curses and sweats, kicks and cusses, just as though his life were on the line.

It is. Ralph's beauty is that he decided to live, and suffer all the consequences. Somewhere along the line he decided this—perhaps in the Marines on a South Sea island. He decided to grab at it, to take it, to taste it, to get everything of it he could. Death was nothing. Life was everything.

How to suggest to him that it might be more than just a piece of dirt? The evidence all points in the opposite direction. When they teach you that mud is your only salvation, they split you in two. Half of you loves life. The other half believes it is dirt.

Anyway, I got up the nerve to ask him for a garden. He gave me a piece of Hank's, a natural-lifer three doors down, and they both helped me get it started, knowing my back was in pretty tough shape. The first day was really painful, but it was good to stick my hands in the earth, to feel it between my fingers as I packed it in around the young tomato and pepper plants. This constantly feeling sick has got to stop or I'll never make it on the outside. The gods that reside in earth and air and vegetation might assist me if I approach them with a humble determination. It's a sad spring, but watching Nature renew itself, seeing that she hasn't yet thrown up the job, gives me a kind of hope that strength might return. I'd really like to send this corset back to G.E. so they can pass it on to the next sucker whose back needs to be done in on the production line of Progress. But first I want to stamp Attica State Prison all over it and then maybe smear it with dung.

Such thoughts are really subversive; I'm glad I don't live in California.

A moment of lucidity, and then the fog creeps in. It's amazing, how misty the nights are up here. Pneumonia country if there ever was any. I don't know if that's a good way to die or not—but I'd just as soon not do it in here.

Perhaps we should be permitted to select our choice of death. It would seem more civilized. There would still be those who would choose the guillotine, the noose, the chair. No one would really be unemployed. But when will they learn that life can be as profitable as death?

Astounding! The very thought is subversive to the whole system, which is organized so crucially to the whole issue. Blood, sweat, and tears may lubricate the machinery, but the trapdoor of history has claimed too many victims. I cannot die with hatred on my fingertips, any more than I can live with it in my heart.

It is the truth.

I can't have a typewriter in my cell, but I can snatch a few moments at my profession here and there on these machines. There're about five of them here, more or less in working shape. Naturally they don't expect me to write anything except illiterate bullshit, my mind having been wiped out by acid. Mr. G. in the next cell is convinced I'm some kind of homicidal witchcraft maniac. A really dangerous case. But maybe he's never understood why anyone would really try to be nice to him.

Especially Whitey.

Rumor is rife there's a mind-destroyer among us. Namely, me. Most of these birds would have given me life. They probably favor capital punishment, too. The blacks hardly speak to the whites, except to give orders. They're into a military thing. That's progress, I suppose. It's hard not to laugh out loud. But the thought of an endless succession of days of this bullshit stops me. It just about stops me.

All that fucking Norman Mailer shit was bullshit. There are no white fucking niggers.

There are no black fucking niggers, either.

There are just fucking niggers.

It's really a term of endearment, come to think of it. Oil Can Hairy proved that back in County Pen. He ran out of his cell on the upper gallery and called them all a bunch of fucking niggers. Everybody was stunned. There were token gestures of making a fight of it, but there was also a degree of fascination with the figure of Hairy, as he liked to call himself, leaning through the bars like a white woolly-haired ape wearing Flash Gordon glasses with lenses so thick you could see Mars though them on a clear night, shaking his fist like a jackhammer over the heads of all the jackasses downstairs.

Hell's Angels' reputation would be upheld wherever he went; no bullshit. Willie was set to grapple him, but the guards moved in, and the whole thing petered out. Everyone was relieved.

The idea of calling a black man a nigger is not so much a put-down as it is a venture in communication. To scale those emotional walls on the stray chance of finding someone on the other side, worthy of having been called Enemy, is truly an adventure for any Knight of the Road.

Now the Reverend D.'s coming over to see what I'm doing at this machine. Guess I'll have to stow this.

Officer O'Sullivan marches us to chow. He's a tragic case, and my heart would really go out to him if I didn't also hate his guts.

Fuck all Irishmen. They're not dumb, they're just willfully stupid. Then, when you least expect it, they show signs of pure genius—blinding you temporarily to their basically atavistic attitude toward life. Which is a nasty thing to say, but when you take a good look at what's happened to O'Sullivan, you can't help it.

Too much Legion Hall. Never enough money, the government always grabbing it to support "these monkeys" and all the welfare deadbeats in that goddamn nigger-city who don't end up here. But it was too late now to change. It was always a toss-up between escape and re-tirement, but the longer you thought about it, the more years you found had already been invested. And for what? A lousy night or two at the Legion Hall, till you were drunk enough to imagine you were really going to enjoy screwing your wife tonight—if you didn't get too drunk to forget you had that idea in mind.

Balls. Everybody Chooses His Own Grave is the theory of this whole society. It would be perfect, only some ass-hole renegade always insists on having a choice of life.

But that's why we have prisons, in essence.

In back of me is Diz and he won't let up. His steady rap is annoying beyond belief. "Man, these goddamn *red-necks*," it begins, and runs from there. His story is he killed a cop. I think he's such a bullshit artist no jury could ever convict him of anything except Sodomized

Humbug. A plea-copper from way back, but talks like a militant. According to him, his main aim in life is to stamp out Whitey. So far, he hasn't really succeeded. Somehow the vicious criminal keeps eluding him at the wrong moment.

Yard talk: "Looks like rain, don't it?" Me.

The trouble is, I don't know how to keep my mouth shut.

"Yeah, man—I'd say it looks like rain. What would *you* say it looks like?"

"Hmmm. Rain."

"Well, solid on that. It does my heart good to see somebody with the same opinion on something. You were in 10 Company in Reception, weren't you?"

"Yeah. I remember you."

"I hope so. There's only one Diz in this institution, man."

"No. There's another one . . ."

"Another Diz? You must be crazy, man—there's *no other* Diz in *this* institution."

He might have been right from his point of view, so I let it pass. A real cop-killer wouldn't even bother with this kind of conversation. Still, he interested me in a way. He was a leftover, a survival from something. Which meant we had something in common. Maybe just the better part of forty years.

"So you're behind me now."

"That's right, brother. I'se *right* behind you, all the time."

"Out of sight. Maybe we should have an understanding."

That really fucked him up. He'd done everything short of calling me "redneck," and here I was proposing a truce. It had to be some kind of sneaky deal—just enough to capture his imagination.

"What you got in mind, baby?"

A quick suck-off in the john could have been my answer, but that would have meant open warfare. And what if I had to put up with that my whole bit?

"Nothing in particular. But when something comes up, I'll let you know."

He thought that one over and softened a little. "You in here for dope, ain't you."

"In a manner of speaking. LSD."

"Huh. I tried that stuff, too."

Bullshit. But I let him have it that way. Maybe sometime he did try it—as though that could have made any difference.

"Really? I never would have thought."

"Oh, yeah. I been there and back, man."

"Solid." Which should have ended the conversation, but I went further, feeling that no matter what I might think about Diz, he is somehow intimately connected with the tone of my existence for the next year or so.

Deadly thought. Yet maybe there is something about him I might like, given time. He wasn't exactly the type you wrote protest songs about. George Jackson might be a brother, but Diz would always end up being slightly on the other side of whatever. And I have no more patience for that.

I have no more patience for anything. It's so easy to get beat in here just for conversation, so you start inventing them.

The alternative is deadly silence. Which convinces everybody you're a whack-job, so they leave you alone for a while.

Nice.

Oil Can Hairy was a better conversationalist. Ollie's shipped out, Wade's on his way to Auburn. It really doesn't pay to make friends in prison. But it doesn't pay not to have any, either.

Diz's militancy sucks. But when he starts rapping about Matteawan, you have to listen. You couldn't avoid it, really, unless you were in another block.

Everybody loves a horror story, and he knows them all—just where the bodies were buried, how much was left of them to bury. I can believe some of them, too. Too many—all you have to do is extrapolate from where this place is at. The Criminally Insane have no recourse to anything; they're at the complete mercy of the state. The state is interested mainly in maintaining sanitary conditions. However, it doesn't always measure up to its own standards. But a high-pressure hose can generally flush the evidence from those occasional off-the-cell-wall scenes. And the standard rule is, Nobody's to blame when emergency situations arise.

Matteawan. Dannemora. "Dig it; I been there and back."

Still, I wish he'd shut up. His voice occupies Cell Study during the day and the gallery at night. Most of the rap is plain ridiculous; on the outside he'd make a good pitchman for the Gay Liberation Front. But Diz is in prison now, so he's got to maintain the militant image: "If you don't take a head, man, you ain't said *anything*, you dig?" Frantz Fanon, going down like warmed-over shit. I refuse to rap with him about race, and this just makes him furious.

What the hell is there left to say about race? You could rack your brains and not come up with anything that didn't sound like parables invented by some dimwit paranoid philosophy student.

Cleaver said it all, but not quite. Maybe he thought a white man couldn't fall in love with a black girl. Maybe falling in love is the special privilege of the underprivileged altogether.

I doubt it. Socioeconomically, love doesn't exist, anyway. It's a fantasy to think that any system can either include or prevent it, let alone control it. Which is why all our convenient categories eventually break down . . .

To love anything, you must be slightly crazy. It's all a gamble of emotions, and this way of experiencing yourself can amount to suicide.

Still it's tried. Every day, and even in here. Stan, in the back of the room, has lost his head over a dark bit of fluff on the second floor. Both handsome specimens, but you can see how murderous a game it is—she has all the advantage. She's black, tall, a high-stepper. Stan lifts weights in the yard, displaying a marvelous physique. But lines of strain are beginning to show on his face. She's too much for him to handle—a real cock-teaser. All the natives are delighted by this game, of course— another bit of spice for dinner conversation.

Today I'm going to try an experiment. I'm going to call somebody up for an interview and see if he really exists. Or I really exist . . .

Three dots are pretentious, some say. Céline used them all the time. But then, he never got busted for acid.

Brown dots were where it was. Right now, I'd take just about anything for relief from this pain.

Who wouldn't?

P.M.

"Hairy's" here and I'm calling him up. I got word to him through the Savage, a truly hairy friend from County Pen, to drop a slip in for a Cell Study course. Should be in tomorrow, I'll call him up then. I'm wondering if he's still decorating his cell with drawings of choppers.

The Hell's Angels thing has some kind of a toehold in here, but it seems like mostly talk. In County, Harry was into sending letters out to Sonny Barger. I helped him compose a few. It seemed like a good idea—who knows when you're going to run into some Hell's Angels.

Harry showed me a photo of his fifteen-year-old red-head from Florida, wearing a swimsuit. If that's what Hell's Angels is about, I'm for it. All the rest of the primitive stuff can be gotten around, I'm sure. After all, there were Vikings who never bloodied a breechclout. Harry might have been one of them, except he was so damn nearsighted. It made everyone want to test him.

Harry could take it. He had brains, too, but the obvious stupidity of the scene always somehow eluded him. There were a few times when I thought we were really going to have it out. But I could never really dislike anyone who turned me on to coke and acid in a county jail. The fact that he got it delivered made me believe some of his shit. He listened to mine, too, but we almost blew it when I told him the only nigger he had to worry about was the one in his head. "If we're going to go any further in life," he said, "you'll have to explain that remark." I was getting adrenalin rushes that damn near incapacitated my vocal chords. He could see it, and it made him laugh—that was the end of that.

How the hell can you hate a Hell's Angel?—provided he isn't swinging something at you, that is. His code is in general more ethical than that of the average businessman. His need for speed may be a shortcoming, but at least he tries to do it in style. And some of those bikes are really beautiful.

Kids. I've dug them from coast to coast. Whatever they were into, I dug it. But some of them made me cry. The ones who had no real idea what they were into, mostly.

Being into a motorcycle is something. Being in love with life is something else. A fearful thing, an incurable habit, an unscratchable itch.

Acid couldn't touch it. All I wanted to do was travel, go everywhere, take real trips, voyages of discovery in the outer world.

The hell with the inner. That's for sick people. It reveals itself in everything you do, and if you don't understand what you're doing you're in trouble to begin with —acid probably won't help you a great deal. You'll probably just have a bad trip and make everybody around you upset.

Like Leary. His trip must have sucked, but he sure fooled a lot of people. If a person could keep his religious agonies to himself instead of trying for a television spectacular, he might really someday manage to change the world.

I don't know if I'll ever take acid again. It all depends on who's doing the offering, I guess. A sweet young chick is about the hardest thing in the world for me to resist.

Won't you look down upon me, Jesus?

Big Mack gave me a play today. He spoke, even grinned! He sits in the back of the room, next to Stan, and the two of them have put in enough time combined to rate the driver's seat.

I had to scotch. Stan's rap in the bud. When he started in about the horrors of acid and the heinous perversity of the acid field, I turned to Teddy next to me and said: "Fuck that bullshit, I've heard it all before."

Whether there was a tense moment or not, I don't know. There are times when you just don't care. Either one of them could probably pick me up with one hand. On the other hand, they might have some problem. Adrenalin rage is a great equalizer.

But let's not think about that. I want to get out of here someday, preferably in one piece. Anything that happens goes down in the record. "Shows tendencies toward violence and antisocial behavior."

And so forth. Women are really my weakness, and I can see that from now on I'm going to have to control it. Just how, I don't know.

They all get to me one way or another. They all have something to say, even the worst of them. And I can never remember not to listen.

It hurts just to think of it.

I started to write about Mack and lost the thread. He's interesting if only because he's so visible. A clench-jawed Irishman, about six three or four, silver-and-gray brush cut, glasses. Be on the lookout. Known to collect jewelry from unaware customers and guests of hotels.

How a thief could be that huge and get away with it is beyond me. Mistaken identification would be impossible, and Mack doesn't look the type for rubber masks, silk stockings, etc.

I think his only motive was to avoid work. This bestows a certain sense of honor in regard to his criminal escutcheon. His views on politics are a little bit right of the Pope's. He'd like to see sterner discipline in the joint, less bullshit. "Hard bits but short bits" is his answer to penal reform. "Hard but *short*."

Probably that's the main complaint with the whole damn system—the amount of time ladled out by all these heavy-handed judges. The rack was kinder so long as you survived it. Your body can build itself again and again if you're determined. But nobody can take away the chill of those years. Nobody can do anything for your head after it's been shot full of holes by a world you tried in your better moments to believe in.

If not this world, then what? So it begins—the real agonizing, which drives you down into the metaphysical roots of your soul.

If not this world, then the next. There's a succession of karma to go through; there are strands and strands of it, dragging at your ankles like pliant chains, following you through the road to eternity.

But it sounds and looks like a chain gang. There must be a way to get off it, to burn the placenta of lousy luck that keeps following you around. It's a loser's psychology, perhaps. But ultimately one may have to dig the truth in it.

How many crimes did I commit in my past lives? How much atonement is necessary? Must I pay it like this, on the installment plan?

ПППППП

The taste of brandy on my lips
The touch of starlight in my eyes,
The sound of someone's voice in love,
The sound of love in sighs,
The sight of love
A night of love
And all its sad good-byes
Are just the kind of things you miss
In a godforsaken place like this.

It'll never get anywhere as poetry, but you have to do something to keep from going insane. I'm having a tough time, and everybody seems to know it. Jerry walks me around and around the yard, steady rapping about the Universal Mind. There's a lot of interest in religion in here, but it's badly mismanaged. Which is to say, little tolerance is exhibited for unorthodoxy of any kind. The Muslims are pressing for their own services and should get them, maybe next year.

It seems to me they're barking up the wrong tree—the same old racist one. It was to be expected, but they've perverted some very good religious ideas in the process, and in such a way that they can only isolate themselves further and further from the mainstream—which is just what the infidel wants. Meanwhile as a group they're tightly knit, well disciplined, clean, neat, and really very boring. In the yard they look like robots, going through their paces. There's no music in it. Yet the Koran is full of music; wild, ecstatic music; passionate music; music of the soul and music of the senses. Some of the most beautiful things said on love were written in Arabic. Reading translations in County Jail, it blew my mind to find out why I had been driven mad . . .

Gogol. Or Barney Google, what's the difference. Society is a madhouse, and if a little blood gets spilled now and then, who can help it. We are busy constructing cartoons of ourselves, constantly. *The New Yorker* perverts all its readers with its prison cartoons. How can those droll people in dungeons really pose a threat to society?

But they do. The proper authorities will just have to handle it somehow. Time for my morning cup of coffee. Maybe today I'll take a ride on the A Train.

The prison is full of A Trains. It's the first thing you hear in the door: "A Train, brother?" The little white pills circulate all over the place, tolerated by the authorities because as long as the prisoners think they're stealing them, they'll keep taking them, driving their heads further into perpetual depression. Keeping the population in lockstep, a slow, slave-type shuffle. The bodies flicker past the windows on their way to evening mess, shadows, mere forms, passing through the twilight of life at its lowest ebb. You can almost hear a steady moaning, low, ethereal, unreal . . .

The chant of the dead-in-life. Whose ears does it reach? Whose restless sleep catches an echo, a reflection, a sad whisper which sets the dreamer muttering, a cry in the night which wakens him in terror of finding himself in some place like this, remote, forsaken, forgotten by everyone who couldn't pay the price of conscience?

God only knows.

And He isn't talking. His countenance remains impassive in the face of all this horror. Those who try to poison the secret springs of existence must pay the price —and what will it be? There may be places left where it is still possible to sleep without hearing a scream in the night, but for how long? The feast of images must eventually glut the minds and senses of the multitude

—what then? Who will manufacture a silencer for the human heart, the pulse of life, the dance of the atoms? Let him lie down in his own grave.

In the meantime we can try not to snivel and whine. Each day has some precious gift if only we can see it. Mack showed me an exercise that seems to be helping my back. Jerry keeps me going with the Universal Mind, which he's worked his way out to through a combination of physics and Christian Science. The Good Doctor D. smiles benignly at his sheep, but the gimlet never really quite leaves his eye. If he'd stop confusing religion with authority, he might actually someday do something. But that would take a lot. Meanwhile he has his divinity degree just in case. And a lot of guards, all armed with Mace.

He got textbooks on criminal psychology, too. He got theories, too. He got courses which change your mind around to the other side, let you see things through the eyes of a normal, law-abiding citizen.

Quite a trip, but don't hold your breath too long.

The Head Nigger in here likes to give me a bad time. He's really something else—quite an actor. Due to go out on parole pretty soon, a Harlem boy complete with goatee and thick-lensed horn-rims and a giggly laugh that recognizes somewhere the preposterous caricature he's presenting: the registrar.

"Coon! Come here!" in a loud, hard voice, and I slowly shuffle my way over, acting dumber than he knows anyone can be. Some tense moments, but we ended up laughing. Today he rapped to me for the first time, telling me funny-money stories from New York City.

They were really funny. I gave him a quick rendition of an acid trip, and the pressure between us vanished. Now I'm going to kind of hate to see him leave, because the new Head Nigger might turn out to be a real son of a bitch. I'm operating independently up here, and everybody's afraid it might conflict with their "thing." But it's the only way I can operate, and if they don't like it, fuck it. I get my lessons out. I'm starting to do interviews, too. But the registrar controls the paper, and the paper controls the prison.

Harry was up this morning—a disappointment. He isn't really into anything, it seems. Not even that crazy "I'm going to grab my mother and fuck her the next time I see her" talk from County Jail. Maybe he's straightening out in here. Rehabilitation is really completely up to the individual; all the authorities have to do is stop fighting it. But they can't. Too many of them make a living off corruption.

That's the clench. Institutionalized degradation always seems more profitable than earnest efforts. I wrote a letter to the commissioner that would have brought tears to the eyes of a heart-transplant surgeon, but my transfer to Auburn was put off. That means it's dead—I don't have that much time. Also wrote to the judge trying to find out why he gave me a different kind of sentence in court from the one they sent me here with. He denied everything. I could write to my lawyer, but it's hopeless. No court is really interested in such technicalities—stay put and shut up, and the Parole Board might give you a break. Otherwise . . .

Otherwise you just foul up your record. The break you might get if you win is just about canceled out by the time you spent getting it. They measure these things pretty carefully, and the consensus is, unless you've got a federal case, forget it.

I was an asshole to get arrested like that, anyway. My real crime was Dealing in Emotional Dynamite. If I'd ever been able to get that little bitch out of my mind for one moment, I might have been able to see what I was doing.

I don't know if she's out yet. She taught me one good lesson: The only mind you can really blow is your own. But in order to learn it, I had to do it. How suicidal that can be is open to question—she was convinced I would, but if for no other reason than that, I didn't.

Harry and I rapped the whole morning, and the Reverend Doctor D. didn't say a word about it. Once in a while he walks down the room, hoping to catch an earful. Something for the office boys up front. We switched in mid-rap from acid trips to motorcycles. But Harry seems relatively subdued here in the Big Place. Not scared, just thoughtful. He's thinking a lot about his life, what he wants to do when he gets out. Like suddenly it's more than just Hell's Angels.

That's good. But he definitely needs the transfer to Auburn. The school here sucks.

They're simply not prepared to cope fully with the idea of educational rehabilitation. It's seen as a failure on the outside, what with college kids rioting and smoking dope (as they say in California)—somewhere along the line dangerous ideas always come to the surface. Teaching history as a war between the good guys and the bad guys doesn't always work, evidently—at least not the way it used to. The trouble is, there's too damn much emphasis on education in this country! What we need is more *training*.

For every problem the same answer. They'll rip themselves to pieces to defend this deadly point of view, but who cares? Mutilated children are unfortunate, but there are always casualties in any war, and there will always be war because there will always be people . . .

Maybe. Maybe such rationalizations can still persist in a world whose chief symbol is the question mark. It hangs over all of us, and all the computers in the world won't remove it. We need to take risks, all right, but not the kind of risks we've been taking. Any gambler worth his salt stays away from loaded dice. The supply of suckers isn't quite so inexhaustible as we've been taught to believe, and nature has a nice way of putting a finishing touch on naïve philosophies.

I really hope Harry drops the Oil Can and makes it someday. He's got a sort of beautiful mind, underneath it all. Something really American there, which means no truckling or knuckling under to all the slobs who want to sell you short, all the assholes who want to grease you up and make you one of them.

Some guys need prison, and it hurts to say it. But they need more than this one is offering . . . On just about any level.

It's only offering death.

If you're sufficiently hated, you can live. Otherwise, forget it.

It was a mistake to shoot George Jackson, under any circumstances. And we all know just how the circumstances were created. By God, maybe, but it's up to us to interpret. And that was about as miserable a job as we've seen yet.

If George Jackson had been running for national office, it might have been different. But all he was doing was being a prisoner, as far as the facts relate. Maybe he was having an affair with Angela Davis at one time. Maybe he had a brother who blew a judge's head in.

Maybe he had piles. Who knows. But you shouldn't dignify the masses this way if your real intention is to render them totally impotent in directing the world's course.

However, if you're stupid, that's just what you'll do, and let the ministers chalk one up for Jesus.

Politicians have a perfect right to shoot each other down, we all know that. But they really shouldn't expect songs to get written in honor of their martyrdom every time it happens. The people don't have the patience necessary for those extended periods of mourning.

When they want something to sing about, they'll think of George Jackson.

Lordy Lord, they'll sing: Lawdy, lawdy Lord!

It's quite true that a convict is actually a piece of ratshit. But that's exactly what makes him so much like all of us. Which, again, is why he must always be such a despised creature. If people ever stopped despising themselves, crime as a distinct category of activity would very likely become insignificant.

But that's part of the game. We need criminals, we need convicts, we need men in prison, if only to help convince us something is under control. Anything. We need them there in case one day we might want to take a good look at ourselves—the selves we thought we had forgotten about. That will be a treacherous day indeed, but even the rich know deep in what's left of their hearts that it can't really be avoided.

Which is why they spend so much money trying. It's their privilege, I suppose, but the brutality so often displayed in defending it indicates paranoia on a massive scale. Outlandish schemes have become a commonplace in their calculations. In the political arena they behave just like the animals they imagine pose such vast threats to all the foundations of their existence. But they are their own worst enemies, architects of their own kinds of doom.

The only thing to do is pray for them, perhaps. The obvious agony of their tremendous, far-flung, and one might mention, farfetched responsibilities seems to be more than they can handle. It's rapidly driving them further and further past the borderline condition into a realm of the psyche that is really uninhabitable for anything human. They appear to have abandoned hope, faith, charity, and even reason.

106

All of which conspires to make them rather unentertaining people. If the Beatles had become American citizens, settled down, and run for office, we might have been spared some of this bad breath. But, of course, the CIA would have to work it from their end.

Of course, of course.

Any day now I may go berserk. But I'll have lots of company. I do right now. Maybe my quarters aren't quite as comfortable as the governor's, but they're sufficient. My only complaint is the lack of heat on these damp, cold days. I really dread the winter. The very thought of it makes me want to stop.

Why did you kill her?

Strange dreams, strange voices. Wake you in the middle of the night, as though someone had whispered the words into your ear. The dim overheads in the gallery provide barely enough light to write by. But that's fitting.

The story of a man in search of the source of his guilt.

It became difficult very early in life to conceive of responses of love toward myself; I nevertheless tried. Reaching out for Chinese oranges and finding them suspended from the lower boughs of a giant oak tree . . .

Extended metaphor. A road leading back to a home I'd never been sure of—not after that night. They said you couldn't go back again, but it seems as though all my life I've been trying to do just that.

It comes to me now: why I wake up like this, suddenly, in the small hours of the morning, so alone, so disturbed—and yet somehow peaceful. I've been dreaming; my body is moist as though from some physical exertion. The night sounds, the wind; something rattles— a garbage-can lid?—out there in the dark that presses against the huge gallery window. But these things are no longer my enemies. They are part of the road that leads me back *there,* the one I know I have to walk.

I really have to make it this time. Dreams are not enough. Touching my fingertips together I can feel my life, the ridges and whorls of it, minute sensations magnifying, time a palpable dimension, plastic.

I set out: a river road winding up through hills which lie in convoluted quiescence, fallow after harvest moons have come and gone—all obtaining to the permanence of a frozen dream-vision.

Hills like the ones around here: low, abrupt, easily able to hide a prison.

I see it all now with a sense of displaced terror. Some truth in what Dr. D. says, but I wonder at it: just how much can any man know about these matters—about the hills, about the river, about the road back home? In the reality we find a dream; in the center of the dream, reality. But only when we dream we are dreaming are we truly awake, it has been said. The landscape will always be there, just as it was: apple trees, cherry boughs, chestnuts, snow not yet on the ground, the world a silent waiting.

Not quite silent, not everywhere. From an ancient clapboard three-story structure where an iron kitchen stove defends the night and the chilling change of season, voices are rising; shouts and cries ring out to offend the ears of slumbering neighbors.

She's drunk. But what is drunk? A disgraceful state, but I'm sure what it *means* to be drunk. My tongue, which never tasted alcohol before *her,* remembers bitterness from an open bottle left carelessly at hand behind an antique dresser—*when?* These investigations took place in dislocated time, between the day when she kissed a startled infant's foot, surprising him with the softness of her lips as he lay in his crib, unprepared for a gentleness he had not seen in her distracted features, and that night, some twelve or thirteen years later—

She wasn't meant for poverty. It had never been conceived of; it was never part of the design; there had never been a plan, just a promise of life eternal, decorated with the sweetness of blossom-covered hillsides in an orchard-country springtime. Winter was Christmas, and the rest you just lived through.

But it hadn't been like that, so she drank. She drank and she did everything she felt like doing, telling the world to go screw.

She had a father, too, and when they finally fought it was an agony of near-murder, their bodies striking the floor, swift and tense and tremendous with the inhuman strength of agonized love. The stove was nearly knocked from its moorings; a vision of flames leaps through my stupefied brain at this incomprehensible spectacle.

A world in flames. Her strength was terrific. Sister, brother, father, mother—son—had to hold the door shut against her, imprisoning her in the second-story bedroom.

It didn't do any good. There was a window; she jumped.

The neighbors didn't take long to call the police, and that was the last I saw of her.

Yes, I see the rain. I've seen it and I see it now, a dull damp drizzle, a mean rain, a soaking rain that darkens the rocks and trees and earth, drenching the landscape without mercy.

I've seen better rains. I've listened to them in better places. The rain that comes today doesn't look so good. Black Spring, Henry Miller called it, and he knew what he was talking about. He came to the prisons, he looked in them, he talked to the convicts, he saw the soul of America rotting in a lime pit. He came because after his journeys of discovery to lands where a name meant nothing, where freedom and anonymity are synonyms, where the soul's voyage is unimpeded by anything except the limits of one's imagination, he could never be free until he'd discovered that part of his soul—the part shoved down in the lime pit.

Some of the convicts are painting pictures in their cells. Others are reading, some are sleeping, some writing, rapping, or listening to their headphones or just staring at the riveted ceiling.

Cell time, Saturday afternoon, no yard, no movie. Reinforced indolence. Now's the time to pull out that letter, the one she finally sent, the one that alarms you so.

"The kids are all right." But you know they're not; you know they're about totally fucked up by the whole thing. Sure, but kids are tough—they'll live through it.

Only why should they have to? Who sentenced them to this? To having a piece of their soul in prison? Was this trip that really necessary?

Whose fault?

Sheer torture. The rain offers no relief; it is the same rain that fell yesterday and the day before, till it became pointless to peer from the third-story window of the school, out over the stark gray wall at the dull hills and farmlands beyond. Pretty country, but it rains a lot around here.

You wish it would come swift and punishing. Lightning should rip apart the sky, thunderbolts come hurtling down. The metal structures act as a ground, current may be going through us; it's a thought, a novelty, hold on to the bars and feel for a tingle of life.

Ralph is in his cell, cursing. No garden today, no greenhouse, fuck it all.

We've got a new neighbor between us, a young kid named Jim, picked up on parole violation while tripping out around the Southern Sierras.

They nailed him in Albuquerque, a real dumb show because he'd been driving the Camper without a license. Had one, too, only lost it up in the mountains on a skiing party with some rich broads from Boston the week before. That's the breaks. There was nothing his friends could really do for him once they'd picked him up; he'd absconded from parole in Boston almost a year before. Still had five to do, too—they might make him bring back a year or more before another shot at the bricks.

They might do anything. The Board is notorious for it's hardhearted hits; this is a Maximum Security Joint, after all. Anyone in here really represents a bad risk for society. Nothing but gorillas in here. Nothing but misfits, apes, monkeys, miscast members of some bizarre black comedy being produced in a white theater of the absurd.

Nobody bad-mouths a convict as mercilessly as another convict. "Dogs, they're all dogs," Jim snarls softly, curling his words with bitterness. "Nonhuman scum, filth!" Ralph the Gardener is in full agreement; if anything, his bitterness runs deeper. But he is older and has had more time to develop it, including the time he still faces.

"They suck," Ralph agrees. "All of them. In Joliet it wasn't like this. No, sir, nothing like these rat-fuckers in this joint. Jim, I've been in *five* of them and never seen anything like this! Nothing like this! These dirty motherfuckers in here wouldn't—Jim, let me tell you something. Let me say this, Jim: Nobody expects the Harvard Club in a place like this. I've been in *Angola*, Jim—it's a *hard* joint. They've buried guys in there. But any goddamn motherfucker comes in that joint learns to deal with his fellow prisoners, not just screw them every chance he gets. These motherfuckers wouldn't make it in Angola. Jim! They wouldn't make it anywhere! They'd try to screw their own mother if there was ten cents in it. And you know what? Most of them would bungle the job, Jim!"

Ralph hates this joint with a passion. His constant rage at it keeps him from having to examine his own rage at himself, most of the time. When he starts doing that, he gets really bad. Glassware might come flying out of his cell. Every day there's a new thing to rage at, but it all amounts to the same thing: this place. His passionate wish is to get back to Joliet. He's still facing a federal rap after this one.

Ralph has always lived by a kind of code, and he can't understand anybody who hasn't. He had the Marines behind him. He had some college behind him, a short stretch which he mostly drank his way through. He never took anybody off who wasn't in one way or another classifiable as a motherfucker. Mainly, he'd worked with checks, credit cards, forgeries. In the printshop at Joliet they'd printed up enough cards and credentials to keep a small army going for an indefinite period. As long as they kept going. Motion was the essence of the hotel-motel-bank-and-finance-company (not to mention department stores and an occasional out-and-out heist if it was right) circuit —motion and a good sense of timing.

So what happens. He gets caught in Cooperstown with a trunk full of paper. Everything you'd need to live off the land. There'd been a fuck-up somewhere, people hadn't gotten together. Nothing left to do but start drinking again. Warrants out for him in four states. What a laugh.

How would you write about a situation like this?

Thinking about that, he got careless, and when they stopped him for running the light, he was surly, so they decided to search the car. Next thing they were down at the station calling up the FBI.

The FBI. That's another story altogether. The dumb motherfuckers were right next to him twice, and he'd been able to talk his way out of it. Sat down in a booth on Eighth with one and had a drink, discussing the whereabouts of one Ralph so-and-so, and he'd damn near pulled the wrong ID out of the wrong pocket. Close, but the dumb bastard had showed him a picture of himself, and he'd had to invent a quick story. "Sure, I know who you mean—I've seen him a couple of times; he does look like me. I think he goes mainly to a bar on Fifty-eighth —I don't remember the name."

"Could you take me there?" the agent naïvely asks.

"Sure I could take you there," Ralph says eagerly. "I'm going that way, anyway. Just wait till I take a piss, will you?"

The agent nods and it's through the bathroom door and out the bathroom window. Some caper. When he reaches the corner and peeks down the block, the guy is still standing outside the bar, waiting patiently.

Walk quickly away from it. Hot as a pistol and it's time for some country. The rest cure. Nerved-up like this, you're bound to make mistakes. Jack will meet you in Oneonta.

Only no Jack in Oneonta. No motherfucking Jack in

Oneonta, and why he'd stopped in Cooperstown he'd never know. Fuck the Baseball Hall of Fame.

The jail was one-horse, and he tried to saw his way out for two weeks. Would have made it, too, except somebody squealed.

Now this place. Full of niggers of the worst sort. They wouldn't give you the time of day if you needed it to make parole. They wouldn't pull together with you on anything. They loved the place just the way it is, because they think they're running it. Meanwhile they rat each other out and fuck each other up the ass. Show them a favor and they'll call you a sucker and find some way to screw you for more.

Fuck niggers.

Fuck everything.

So it goes with Ralph. He's about given up, but not quite. The garden keeps him busy. Gambling takes up the slack. There's pinochle in the yard, there's occasional sets of bridge. There are the baseball tickets, the football tickets, the basketball tickets. Every real sports-lover is a gambler. It was easy to make up a bank and start with your own tickets. But not in this joint. The dumb motherfuckers came up with bullshit that was beyond belief. Stupid shit, to get out of forking over a few lousy packs of cigarettes on a penny-ante bet. So you played their tickets, and if they tried to beat you, you'd find some way to screw them.

Some goddamn way to keep from going crazy and being sent to HBZ again. That had been a bad scene, but he'd do it again if somebody tried to fuck him.

It had been Donny, the white farmboy from rural upstate, up for shooting his brother dead with a hunting rifle. Ralph had wanted the water-boy job then, carrying hot water to the cells after evening lock-up. It had been promised to him, but Donny had pulled strings, dropped a few tabs. He was sure of it. Sure enough to corner him in the yard and proceed to beat the living piss out of him. It hadn't gotten very far; the hacks had broken it up. A month in the Box and he was back on the gallery, working in Cell Study. which he hated.

The dishonesty of it, the stupidity of it—which was worse? You couldn't run a school that way, with little scraps of shit they called lessons. And every time you came up with an idea to change something, begin a new course, start a prison newspaper, a literary magazine—anything —the phony bastard up there just gave you a tolerant smile and shrugged. You wouldn't get anything out of him, out of any of them.

They didn't know the meaning of the word "give."

It's a pity when we take each other's love and forget to give any back. The sin of indifference covers us all with that kind of guilt. But how many have examined what love has to do with even the simplest act of giving?

It's the hardest thing in the world to see, most of the time, for most of us. When a child gives you a smile, he is giving you a smile. Not permitted in the adult world. A smile is a defense, a mechanism, an act of aggression.

But I see other smiles, other kinds of smiles, in the mess hall. Today for the first time since I began this bit I found myself the only white at a completely black table. Charlie, across from me, grinned and said: "We're going to take your head, Coon. We're going to eat you up at this table."

I gave him a smile. That was all he really wanted. The conversation lit up, and nobody smiles the way a black man smiles when he's really smiling. They dig me because I never try to be one of them. And they know I've dug them, and the rest is just so much bullshit.

They have that much feeling, that much sensitivity. I never rap with any inmate except as an equal. If he doesn't prove to be equal, then I just don't rap with him again. But that doesn't happen very often. Rarely, if ever.

The bad trips show up in the eyes first, and if you keep yours open, you can see them coming and avoid them.

Meanwhile I go anywhere in the yard I like except into the Muslim camp. They've got their own set of tables staked out as a mosque. My curiosity about what they're into stops at the "door." I was in the Army once, I'm not interested in all that militant shit. To me they seem to be intentionally destroying their individuality for the sake of another set of mad abstractions. And who wants to rap with a robot? May Allah preserve them, and me, too.

Mostly it's around the yard with Jerry. He's a funny character, no lie. What he hints about himself is a lot more interesting than what he tells you. A successful production engineer in real life, an itinerant metaphysician in this one. I run him a set of Indian philosophical ideas, and he runs me back his discovery of Purpose in the Universe.

The Universal Mind is where it's at. A force behind the material which manages to keep the atoms dancing. A power that can be tapped if one is willing to really go into it. Christian Science has the key, the outline. Jerry's figured out the rest. All things are possible, given a true recognition of, a realization of, a proper relation to, the Universal Mind.

"You see that wall over there," he points, squinting toward the bricks across the yard. "I believe I can walk through that wall if I really want to."

"Why don't you do it?" I say slyly.

He just laughs. "Oh, I'm not ready yet. There's a lot more I have to go through before I walk through that wall."

I have no idea what that might be in his case. He appears to have brains, personality, energy, drive, self-confidence—all the qualities necessary to success. Why is he in here?

A woman, naturally: "She wouldn't stay away from

117

me. Once my wife and I split up, this bitch kept coming around, coming to the house, she wouldn't stop. I tried to shoot her once. She was driving me crazy, but the gun jammed."

"That was the Universal Mind at work," I suggested.

"It sure as hell was. And that's why I'm here—to understand that fact. This is bad, a bad, bad place. But I'm also glad I passed this way. I had to learn certain things . . ."

Forty-two, and still learning. He learned law in the library and came up with a *coram nobis* that had everybody shook, from the D.A. on up. They were ready to make deals. He'd get this whole thing squashed eventually—they hadn't done a thing right in his case from the moment of arrest.

His ambition is to sail around the world in a boat he was going to start building as soon as he was paroled, which was only a few months away. I really believe he might make it. But he has no use for literature, and this puts me off a bit. I don't know why. Sometimes literature puts me off, too. But I charge that to graduate school.

Right now it's a salvation. I got hold of *The Idiot* from the school library, and it's an interesting translation but makes me read slow. It might take me months to finish.

Good. I've got months. Possibly another year's worth of them. This is only June. I've been here three months and it seems like forever . . .

JULY

The Fourth is supposed to be the Day.

Rumors are spreading like weeds in an abandoned city dump. Which is just about where it's at.

Jerry says No, as though he'd received a message from the Universal Mind. Maybe he's right; everything seems under control in D Yard, but you never know what's coming out of all the other blocks. And they open all yards on the Fourth; it's traditional inmate-visiting day.

Speaking of visits. I guess I'm going to have to go through this bit without one. It grips my guts sometimes when they call the others up out of the yard. I go stand in front of the television set and try to forget about all that. Even in here, TV can be used to narcotize the mind.

Harry's come to D, but they won't be keeping him here; he's on his way to Auburn. Had enough pull on the outside—his lawyer wrote a tough letter to the Commissioner.

"Come to Auburn," he says, "this place sucks like a mother."

"They turned me down the first time."

"So try again. Have your wife phone Albany, anything."

"She's divorcing me. I got the papers last week."

"Oh, shit."

It's an old story, and I didn't bother to tell the rest of it.

But somebody should tell it, somewhere, sometime. It has to be told, if only because it's typical. The plot goes like this:

John loves Mary. Mary loves John. So they get married, and being rather reckless types, have kids. The kids turn out to be very beautiful, so beautiful it begins to scare John every time he sees where the bank account is after all the bills have been paid—which is nowhere, and all the bills haven't even been paid.

So he begins to think of extra ways to get money—just enough to get them economically out of the hole, of course. If he's a teacher and can write three words, maybe he moonlights a sex novel or two. Nice gravy there, and if you have to explain it someday to the kids, they'll probably just laugh at you. You treat them right, regardless. Kids are what it's all about, or if not, then it isn't really about anything, in which case it doesn't matter what you do so long as you stay out of jail. So let's keep it legal.

Keeping it legal isn't so hard, even though you have to deal with slave-driver agents who treat you like a back-door visitor every time you try to see them. But it's better in some ways than selling used cars after supper. Or if you're a mailman, painting flats as scab labor. Or maybe you're a cop, and you're finding ways to sell a little dope without getting burned.

Sure. It's the system. Nobody has a real job, nobody's really doing what he's doing.

We know how it is, and it's always excusable unless you get caught. Even then, it may be excusable as long as you don't get caught *short*. Short of money, short of friends, short of power, short of status—short of whatever it is that it takes to keep you out of the gears of the machine, once you fall.

The machine needs victims. The Bloody Sacrifice Machine needs a constant input of victims. On any level it needs victims, and the succulent, fleshy roots are where it gnaws the hardest, devours with maximum efficiency. Crime in the streets is necessary to keep people off them, to keep them isolated in front of their television sets, full of the illusion of being informed.

The masticating populace chews up this gruel and never really decides to change anything, because it is really all very stupefying. It is all too much, and by the time you've decided something should be done, it's time to turn in—or else you'll never be able to face the grind again next day.

This way the machine extracts years from those who don't fall overtly into its clutches—years that can never be replaced, years that should have been lived instead of just watched, years that should have reaped real rewards instead of just fringe benefits. And as you are slowly driven mad, as quiet desperation gives way to audible fits, tantrums, spells, perhaps even experimentation with other modes of living, the kinds that invite crucifixion, resisting temptation of any kind becomes a meaningless enterprise. When the trapdoor finally flies down away from the soles of your feet, you are almost glad. You knew it was coming, you couldn't stand the suspense.

Hence, "Guilty, your Honor!" You are ready to shout if from the rooftops. But it hardly makes a line in the local newspaper, and that's just the final humiliation.

Before total humiliation. And then, indifference.

Once you become totally indifferent, you will be tolerated again—it is necessary. The individual who cares can be used, too; but it's often an expensive process.

Mary really cares about John, but she has three kids and no prospects; there's a recession. So she goes on welfare.

Welfare is warfare. Welfare is the warfare of the system against the individual. All the hue and outcry is a smokescreen. The system can't do without it; too many jobs are at stake, too much paper work. So we create another category of the despised.

A woman on welfare with a husband in jail awaiting judicial processing had better just as well forget him. She's married to something else now—a system so vast and pernicious the issue of meaningful survival becomes totally aborted. Survival is a matter of satisfying the machine, of obeying *its* dictates, of doing what *it* wants.

"Bury him!" it commands. "This is no longer a man, it is an example of failure! To punish it is just, for we cannot tolerate failure in a society so perfect as this!" At a later date, perhaps, things can be settled up; if the victim still survives, he can be made to pay—through the courts—for all the damage he has done, all the evil he represents. Meanwhile we'll send you a check twice a month.

So shut up. You know your husband's a dirty bird, a declared enemy of sassiety! Besides which, the family court judges, the lawyers, the probation office clerks, all these perfect people, they have to make a livin' too, don't they? Yo' husbin' nah, he really don't deserve to live, messin' 'roun' with that there mind-destroyin' drug, iffen we'd a-let him go, next thing he'd be sellin' it to all the little chillun in the schoolyard! Yew got anythin' good to say about him now? We can make it easy for you iffen yew cwoperate, honey . . .

Then agin, iffen yew don't . . .

Of course, Mary loves John, but she loves her children, too, and survival has been posed to her as a mean decision. The general ethos of kill or be killed. Who does she have to protect her now? The Department of Welfare, the Family Courts, the National Society for the Castration of All Males over Twenty-One.

Dig a little grave in your mind and lay him in there. Otherwise they might cook up something on you, too— un Unfit Mother, married to a Dopester: we got homes for the kids of parents like that.

"The government has an interest in your children," my lawyer said to me in County Jail. If there hadn't been bars between us, I might have gone up on a murder-one rap. You can dignify it any way you want, but in this book there is no way.

The tension mounts.

Maybe there'll be a riot, maybe there won't. Anyone want to take bets?

No takers. I don't think it's going to happen, myself —not this time. The mood in the yards gets surly enough —there could always be a spontaneous explosion—but nothing's together. The militants aren't in command of anything except their own little groups. Personal prestige is still the item that is sought after in here, which is quite a joke.

Monstrous ego trips abound. A turn around the yard reveals the underside of everything, the hind end of the horror show we like to call society. Leftover dingbats from Desolation Row, sleepy-eyed crocodiles, dinosaurs and lizards, and now and then a more frightening look at the face of the twentieth century—strictly limited.

Cracked faces, full of misbegotten pain, full of sin, full of indifference. The weeds cast out from the garden, the hopelessly lost, the violently determined to live anyway. Morality was never an issue, just survival. Man, you some kind of a fool? What's right is what *feels* right! What's left is what they toss us under the dinner table.

A few scraps, just enough to tease. But the feast is going on somewhere, and if you're hip, you won't be standing there with a fork when it rains soup. You'll be standing on the corner, getting yours.

Crimes of violence? There are no such things in a violent society, man. There is only getting or getting took. Getting took is the mark of a fool, without even a crown of thorns to dignify it.

The down-home niggers collect about the tables in the shithouse area of the yard and play cards. They're the only real people in here, and they know it. The rest are all trying to advertise themselves as something more than utter assholes. But you and me, we know.

Willie's getting transferred to Auburn, so he can get visits from his people. Ollie and Wade are both gone. These were cool heads, the yard will suffer without them. The hard-liners on both sides will eventually have their day.

But will it be the Fourth?

I can't really believe it. And yet I know it could happen. Everybody knows. In the meantime there's baseball, handball, cards, and letters. Everybody's got something to do, nobody really wants to upset his scene.

Nobody really wants to rock the boat. To everything, for everything, there is a season. A time to dance, a time to stomp. A time to love, and you know the rest.

It's worth it, God, every second. Let us be destroyed, but let us know that our destruction is in Thy Greater Glory. Only then can we find some peace in life.

Heavy shit. But you think it in here.

A year since the day of my arrest. What kind of thoughts should I be having today?

Grim, as usual. But there are certain things to be thankful for if you look hard enough. Not groveling-thankful, let's hope, but if you can put your mind in the proper perspective, you have to consider the miracle of daily bread, of sun, of just plain air to breathe. These perfect gifts didn't come from man, and besides, I have a place to lie down when I'm tired. It's better than County Jail—a chance to see the sun when it finally does come out. There were no windows in County. Eight months of that, with only an occasional peek at the sky from the exercise cage on the roof, and you find yourself staring with a certain rapt fascination at the flight of birds.

Freedom. A word written on the wind by the tip of a sparrow's wing. This much has been allotted to us, this suggestion of infinity's backdrop against our tentative and temporary struggles to seize upon a single idea that will elevate us beyond these gray walls.

Such an idea has always been searched for, in prisons and out of them. It may be an illusion, but such illusions are necessary to life. Prison is a good place to start thinking about the idea of freedom, to search for the roots of meaning contained in the word.

Many will maintain there is no such meaning; that words themselves are lies, once uttered. Such arguments are clever, sometimes satanically so. If it's true, as Buber maintains, that somewhere in life everyone makes a conscious choice between Good and Evil, then we can only view the spectacle, without giving in finally to feelings of nausea and horror, with something like the Eastern sense of detachment which permits us to offer prayers of thanks even as we are being sacrificed.

But the average American isn't going to go for that. Despite all our efforts at mass education, he hasn't been trained for it. What he's been trained for is a hodgepodge of reactions to a system he'll never entirely understand. To understand the system in its entirety, you have to be filthy rich.

Most of us aren't. Most of us didn't start out with any of the advantages, and let's not talk about color, for God's sake. Let's talk about tangibles.

When I think about America, I feel like a wounded deer. I feel like a poisoned salmon. I feel like a parent, and that's even worse.

Once you have kids, you have a stake in the system. That's if you live with them for any length of time. Below a certain income level, it doesn't pay. A man on the loose has more of a chance. If you stay, they'll have your ass in jail, one way or another.

So. Here we are, and nothing's happened, to speak of. So why speak?

They threw the door open at breakfast, as usual. Air of anticipation, but what were the other blocks up to? Would there be, or wouldn't there? To let these maniacs mingle might be fool's folly; to let them fraternize might mean murder.

Nevertheless, the authorities would risk it—the weight of tradition as heavy on their shoulders as the leaden epaulets of mythologized naval commanders. Reinforcements were brought up, tear and pepper gas staked out at strategic points. It was really an experiment in democracy, they could always say.

Who could always say? Who would have to answer? Riot conditions in this prison are nothing new; many heads had been together trying to figure out why it hadn't happened before now. The desperate search for whatever it is you happen to be doing right.

Sad.

The morning was preparation. Ice from the commissary, crews working overtime to manufacture the simplest types of setups. Yard-crew instruction, last-minute reminders to the uniformed heavies who would guard the entrances to adjoining blocks. Look out for the man who acts drunk or suspicious. Be ready when they come in waves. Try to notice any militant activity, see if you can hear what they're saying when they go through. But most of all, show them you mean business. We've got to keep the interior open on the Fourth or they'll think we're no longer running a model prison . . .

What's dismal about it is the lack of music.

> We have lost the time
> That was so hard to find,
> And I will lose
> My mind
> If you won't see me . . .

That kind of music. You don't hear it in here, not even when they pipe in the sounds from local stations over the yard horns.

> Oh, Mama,
> Can this really be the end?
> To be stuck inside of Mobile
> With the Memphis blues again . . . ?

Immobile, he meant. Just the way you feel in prison. Much motion, but no moving.

The Glorious Fourth broke with a star-spangled sunrise. We got up, we went to chow. "Line it up!" the hack shouts from behind the lockbox at the end of the gallery. A new guy, doesn't know the ropes too well yet. So he has to shout twice as loud. act twice as tough. Which meant that the academy had failed again, or something.

But it was a truly Glorious Fourth, a Fourth like no other Fourth, a day to be remembered, and then, perhaps, forgotten.

The yards broke open well after the noon chow. Some madwoman had designed this prison, a frustrated bitch of an architect who admired twelfth-century cloisters and decided you could throw together four prison blocks that way, and maybe some of these unholy fuckers of mothers would one day see the light. For those who hadn't really deserved to see the light of day, it could be a steel womb, faced with red brick, sullen behind its turreted castle wall in the soft swampy land of a misbegotten little valley where many a lonely frontiersman had spat his lungs out from bronchitis. A perfect place for a prison! someone must have said, and they began filling in.

Rumor has it that one of the major faults of the Northeast runs directly under here; there had been an earthquake years back; doors of an entire block had sprung open, scaring the shit out of those hacks familiar with biblical prophecies, who perhaps muttered prayers as they fled along with their more jaundiced brothers who simply didn't care to be around when payback time came, no thank you.

The doors of the prisons shall open. The lowest shall become the highest.

But only the inner doors opened today, not the outer doors, and as for the rest, well . . .

Jerry and I put on our white shirts for the occasion, deciding to tour the blocks together. His bit is just about over and he wants to see if some of the friends he made in the other blocks are still around to say good-bye to. Meanwhile it may be my last chance to communicate with the Universal Mind for a while—at least, this particular manifestation of it.

We wait in our cells an appropriate amount of time —the time needed to remind us these are jealous and angry gods who dispense these favors. Then it's lineup in the gallery, and some of these dudes are really fixing to eat. Smuggled chicken from the mess, cantaloupes, watermelons, all kinds of crap. First we go to the commissary with our tickets for ice cream, cake, or whatever we ordered two weeks before. More marching through the tunnels, more lineups. Then, finally, yard.

The idea of having a celebration here is in itself deadening. A tree would help, a bush, a clump of weeds, anything. The barrenness of the Gobi Desert has yet to match this. And as for the doings, it's all pretty rickey-tick, a fabulous dream of having fun like back in the old days.

Still they cling to it. Still they need it—the long tit from Mama. Ice cream and cake, a bottle of pop, and what the hell, it's the Glorious Fourth.

Meanwhile, undercurrents. Riptides and undertows, a hell of a lot of subterranean feeling. We get hooked up right with the guys in B, everything's going to go. Yeah, man, but dig what's happening—we're going to have to include Whitey, maybe.

Naw, don't say that. That motherfucker's kept us back just too damn long and you know it.

I dig, but it's not the same. I rapped with some really hip dudes lately. I mean, they're *into* things.

Man, motherfuck the motherfuckers. What they into?

Drugs, for one thing.

Yeah, but like the chickenshit stuff.

No, not anymore, man. They diggin' hard shit, too, now.

So it come back home. Man, let the motherfuckers destroy themselves.

Yeah, and us with it. Say it like it is, we got to make some kind of do.

Sounds like nursery rhymes to me, bro.

Snow White was a freak for dwarfs and you know it. Let's at least dig what these cats got to say.

I ain't got nothin' but time, bro!

Around the quad a couple of times and then the doors were thrown open.

Not without fanfare. Four hacks on a door, and they made sure everybody knew they were tough before turning the key. They made sure of that and cast such bad vibes I began to think again of Riot.

It was in the air. They were using the whole joint as nothing but a training ground in riot-control. Money had come down from higher up for this, and for nothing else. If a disturbance could be handled in here, it could be handled Out There.

Out there where the flag waves freely. Assaulted, tattered, torn, burned in some cases—but still waving. Cops in country towns now wore it plastered on their shoulders. Let 'em tear this one down, they thought, handing out parking tickets with a special feeling of more-than-usual mission, as though Vengeance and Patriotism were at last to unite themselves under a National Banner, and who was more likely to set the motherfucker waving than the present First Citizen?

We'll handle these black cocksuckers, boss—just you wait and see!

Some of these kids had Viking blood in them. Generally, they kept their mouths shut.

The real nigger-beater is the guy who's had to see himself as one, at some time or another. The Irish cop and the Harlem Black Man used to be good friends, at one time—simply on the basis that they clearly understood how much they hated each other. It was seldom anything personal. "He's a good nigger," they'd say of one hip dude, standing on a corner where he knew they were sure to see him, fingering his dong and smiling softly into the neon night glare. "Yeah," his partner would say. "Aces. But I'd hate to have to take him on sometime in a dark . . ."

"Fuck that shit. You're as good as ten niggers, remember that."

"Yes, *sir!*"

"Say it loud!"

"YES, SIR!"

"You're a good kid. Ever think of making the detective squad?"

Mack isn't even coming out of his cell for the occasion. This is his fourth bit, and he's been lucky, and he knows it to the point of getting some religion. As Irishmen go, he's the salt of the earth, but not many people would know it. He doesn't let them—he's a mean mother, and

132

anybody who wants to deny it better look at the size of his right hand. His fingers are as strong as cobras, and he could do the job just as efficiently. He's a real leader up in Cell Study—the type who only does it so he can have a little peace. He sees me as a threat to all this on the one hand, but on the other it's demeaning to see something six times smaller than you as a threat.

That's his hang-up. When I look around me, I see myself as dead, and it's demeaning to think such a state can possibly be disturbed. By anything.

I was going to write about the Fourth and what happened.

What happened was nothing.

But I chose to write about it anyway, so why stop. It's all just a pretext, and we all know it. There are only two classes in this society: taxpayers and criminals. Some of the latter are still at large; most of them have fled to the refuge of public office. The smarter ones are retiring in Texas. Once it's understood that Texas is an illegal state, they'll be doing another kind of land-office business. Every lone gun in the country will blow his brains out just to get into that army. He'll do it with the pride of one who knows he sacrificed nothing for his country, except maybe his asshole, which wasn't that big a deal to begin with. Right?

But let's not be bitter about the Fourth. Back when we were kids, it really used to mean something. It meant quivering vibrations in the gut, because you knew your head was going to be done in by really strange sights and sounds; distant relatives might even come over to dig the fireworks. Uncle Don and Aunt Sal, they used to come by once or twice a year just to check how far down the ladder you were sliding. Aunt Olive was reputed to be a millionairess. Her presence was mostly ghostly. Actually, she'd died a virgin.

Certified. You'd never believe the way they carried

on at the funeral. The West Tuaghkanic Klan of Witches came down to march in the big parade. They wore uniforms of white and blue and passed as the Ladies' Auxiliary. It was good to see them, even if you wondered what the fuck they were doing there in the street in front of your house.

It was good to see anything, then. The dry rot had only begun to set in, and nobody was paying that much attention to it. Norman Rockwell efficiently erased it out for those who read weekly magazines. It was sort of a status symbol to have them delivered.

Yes, I remember America. Ice-cream cones and a bawdy beer party downstairs; nights as thick and heavy as cheddar cheese and stout, days as warm and lazy as the buzzing in a brain numbed by the song of the seven-year locust. Apple trees, too.

It's really a frontier town, America. All it needs is a marshal and a glass of beer and a good old sawdust fart to keep business going. And maybe a nigger or two.

Don't really matter what color.

AUGUST

Time flies on leaden wings. And if that's purple prose, so's my prick. It really aches for some pussy.

⊓⊐⊓⊐⊓⊐⊓

What's really a drag is, they close the school down for the summer—through August into September.

So they dump us into the yard; only the Important People are able to sneak over to the school on special assignments.

I wonder how many of them are working for the Parole Board. There have been cases here where convicts have actually made out the recommendation form for the Board. Not everybody got recommended.

The power structure in the school, inmate, is plain to see, which is why I chose to ignore it. Which is why I am sitting out in the yard, under the blistering sun, writing this nonsense. I'm not even asking them if I can go cultivate my garden. I'm sorry for the tomatoes, but maybe their quiet shrieks of pain will help wake some-body up to the fact that nature is being held prisoner in this damn place. I don't mean just my cock, either.

Although that may be a large part of it. People are beginning to tolerate me now as a somewhat affable weirdo-intellectual with a certain degree of nerve. Only Mr. G. suspects I am actually a violent revolutionary madman. I've had no real scrapes in here, but some close calls.

Not many of those, at that. Most of these guys just want to talk, and I'm a fair listener. I don't get really uneasy till it looks like they're fixing to spit in my eye. I've been identified with just about everything in here, because I talk to everybody, from Nazis to Bolsheviks. There is always some part of their rap I can dig if I can keep them on an individual level. I'm not to be converted, and I guess they know that.

Though I did go see the priest. The funny thing is, I can't remember a word he said. He looks stern, worried, and half crazy. A Slavic accent, or perhaps Greek. Orthodox, naturally. He lent me a book on Catholicism, and I sent him a thank-you note.

It's really pitiful the way these people find it so impossible to loosen up and act human. Each of them has a textbook in his mind called *How to Behave around Prisoners*. Never relax. Always be observant, but try to wear a smile when possible. Keep a good distance; if you for some reason can't, keep on your toes. Never touch a prisoner except when on special occasion a handshake seems to be in order, such as at the end of an interview. Best to have the desk between you, then.

And so on. But formality extends down into the ranks of the inmates, too. The longer a man's been in the joint, the more there is of it, as a rule. Mr. G. treats me with a certain deference, but he's always on the point of exploding. He doesn't like the way I circulate so freely; he doesn't approve of the way everyone seems to rap with me.

There were clear lines of demarcation when he came in; exact measures of status, rules and procedures and forms to be observed, even among the brethren. You learned them all the hard way, and they were good because after you learned them you knew just where everything was at in the whole joint, and you could play the game like a real player, not just another dumb nigger who got caught. Then this little white prick comes in and acts like there were no such things as rules and after four months still gets away with it. He doesn't do anything wrong, but he doesn't do anything right, either—and the rules say you got to do something right, too. But just wait, the fucker will fuck up . . . they all do, sooner or later.

If I don't read the regulation book, it's because I'm doing my own regulating. They have their program, I have mine. Not always sure just what it is, but these exercises seem to be helping my back considerably. Scientific, part of hatha-yoga, which only lately has received some approval from the scientific establishment. Nature may have some value after all, they reluctantly admit . . .

But the bitch of it is being in this yard for a month. The sun blasts down like an angry god; joggers trot by on the pavement, softballers hurl cannon shots at the catcher, weight lifters grunt and sweat and pose for the passing fancy pants, somebody's doing chin-ups, the card tables are busy, the TV watchers stupefied, the hacks half-dozing in their lifesaver's chairs.

What do you want to know? Judo? Karate? How to chop a head off with your little fingernail? Come on in, brother, come on in! This place would make a wonderful health resort, but they'd have to remove most of the weather, which runs from lousy to outrageous. A most inhospitable part of the planet, to be sure.

But the time drags like an agony of chains, each day a link in the seemingly endless forced march of time. To be doing nothing like this is to beckon all the known diseases of the psyche to the mind, where they might sprout, flower, and generate. A lot of these guys seem to be in training for their next getaway, here, under the blazing guns of August.

It's too hot to write.

SEPTEMBER

ⅎⅎⅎⅎⅎⅎⅎ

It's a long way to it, let's hope we get through it.

OCTOBER

Well, the persimmons are probably browning on the coasts of Algiers. But are there really persimmons there, and do they really brown?

Perhaps only the CIA knows. In here things only gray. My hair, for instance—I might come out a shocking white. But there's always hair dye and plastic surgery and shots to make your sex glands tremble with bullish vitality.

But that's only for those who've been successful in the market. Jim, next door, has a few shares in Polaroid. He watches it avidly; in the back of his mind is a homestead up in the Vermont hills. He can do anything with his hands, his friends are holding down the land, all he needs is a fair shot at parole. Here's a kid with every chance of making it and no use for humanity whatsoever. Which means he might make it. Previous prison experience has taught him to be hard and calloused, but he somehow remains sensitive underneath it all, even artistic. He writes well and has a grip on his imagination, most Mr. G. on my other side really hates it when we get into that kind of drug rap.

"So you never shot smack, huh, Mr. Coons?"

"Well, one time. This kid insisted the reason I wouldn't was because I was scared to. So I did, but I didn't like it."

"You didn't dig it?"

"To me it was a down. Besides which I hate needles or anything like that sticking in me."

"To get your pleasure, you must have pain, Mr. C."

"Maybe, if we go grabbing after it. But if it comes naturally, I don't think so."

"How does it come naturally, Mr. C.?"

"When you live natural. But don't ask how to do that, because most of it's against the law."

The sound of a toilet flushing interrupts our conversation. Then the sound of two toilets flushing. Then three, then four.

Pretty soon, everybody's flushing toilets. This could be the start of something. By a prearranged signal, some two thousand inmates flush their toilets simultaneously. The prison disappears, and the country is inundated by a tidal wave of convict shit.

This most profane of civilizations has come to its natural conclusion at last.

NOVEMBER

It's changing.

You can feel the subtle vibrations, but right now they don't add up to much. Right now it's winter, and the main thing is to keep warm, keep well.

Snow already—what will it be like in December? January? Fuck February and March—if you're still standing, you might make it.

The doctor—the medical doctor who presides over sick call—is grotesque. The only thing he'll do is mark you down for five days' cell time, and it's a lot warmer up in Cell Study.

Things are hopping there. The Rev. Dr. D. is getting ready to vacate his position, most probably in favor of a black man. The only black man in the institution qualified is the Reverend ———— ————, a Baptist minister from the Deep South who managed to get some of his education up North. He's a humdinger—I hope they send him up. Race relations in Cell Study are at an all-time high—I don't see what he can do to upset it.

I've jumped up to high-school- and college-level courses, and it's turning out beautiful. I get only the cons who feel like thinking a bit.

It's all just to have something down on your record when you go before the Parole Board, of course. Everybody knows that. Meanwhile I get to rap with people who've been through all walks of criminal life.

They all have one thing in common—a certain amount of undisguised arrogance. They at least know who they are.

148

The place is changing, and I don't know into what. A lot more young people seem to be coming in. It used to be known as an Old Man's joint. Elmira took all the kids, Auburn the in-betweens. But everything that's been established here has had to bear the impact of the population explosion, just like outside.

Now we've got a Mad Bomber. When Harry first pointed him out, just before his boat to Auburn, I thought it was just another freak recently released from the ancient bowels of downstate madhouse prisons, a guy who, like Diz, had worked his way out of the psycho wards of Matteawan to a decent perch in a fairly well-run joint like Attica.

Attica's rep among the old-timers is pretty good. They used to feed better, they used to be stricter, and there was a lot less bullshit. Of course, now there was more freedom . . .

I really want to find out what that means. I suppose, lacking the availability of young women, it's the closest thing you can have in here to a passion.

But maybe I shouldn't dignify it. This much I know: I feel a lot freer than I used to.

Maybe because this is the midsection of my bit, and I still haven't folded. Maybe it's yoga.

If you don't work with your mind in here, you stand a good chance of losing it. If you haven't any, you've found yourself a home.

Jim, the young violator in the cell next to me, loaned me the book *Yoga, Youth and Reincarnation* by Jess Stearn. Two thirds of it is occupied with sales pitches for yoga based on Famous People Who Practice Yoga, as Encountered in Places You're Never Likely to See Unless You're as Harmlessly Hip as Jess Stearn—which is a long time to take to slam somebody.

But the diagrams in the back are good, very explicit. I've been working at it almost six weeks, and my lower back is starting to stay away from the forefront of my consciousness.

That's something. Big Mack showed me simpler exercises, using the bars, which is what got me started. But when Jim laid the book on me, I decided it was time to either take this stuff seriously or forget it.

I can't help it, there's some kind of sweet thing that comes up in me, often at the moment I'm feeling just about absolutely barren. I've wandered about with my mind completely whacked, my sense of direction leading me toward total destruction, or at least it seemed so at the time. Wired, rewired, and wiped out.

I think I'll get back into some yoga. It's going to be tough—a lot of times I'd just as soon jerk off. But there's so little privacy in here . . .

Jim fools around with the harmonica and does a fair imitation of Bob Dylan, but with five times the acid.

He may be one of the few true success stories of the Psychedelic Revolution. Some call it the Greening of America, but I call it the Blackening. A spade's reluctance to go near a tab of acid is matched only by his total acceptance of the experience once he does—which is something few white experts can claim. Wade did it and came out Wade, a truly beautiful spectacle. It really isn't for people who aren't sure of themselves unless they've got a lot of time to do a lot of searching. Maybe that's why dropping pure acid's become the sport of millionaires. I hope it does them some good . . .

In the meantime they should stop busting misguided people like me. I had sort of a belief in the Revolution, before Ed Sanders took it over. Sure, it helped create Charles Manson, but so did everybody who never even heard of it. Satanism is horrible enough, willful ignorance in command is chilling. When they made marijuana a felony, they encouraged everyone to go down the drain on a Chinese junk. LSD is a dangerous drug, but only to people who are dangerous to themselves. That includes too many, I suppose.

Jim blew grass and dropped acid with some very exclusive people during his year or so of abscondence. If he'd been in on a dope bust, it might have been embarrassing.

Embarrassing as hell, to somebody. Well-to-do Bostonians, whose children preferred to take their risks with substances other than alcohol. Perhaps they'd seen too many chronic alcoholics in too many sexually segregated prep schools to believe everything that was told them. At any rate, if the acid was pure, you didn't have to warry about overdosing. The custom in this part of Boston was to have a tab or two before lunch, then let the day work itself out.

Now some of these people seem to be sticking by him. It's a miracle if there ever was one. Jim has some nice acreage up in the Vermont hills, waiting for him in his name when he gets out. He gets a visit every month. He can afford his surly cutthroat cynicism, but I wish he'd direct it away from me. If he's ever able to get his head straight, he might turn into something beautiful. But he cells next to Ralph and works under him in the garden, and any move I make is bound to be interpreted as hostile. I have no Big Crime stories to tell.

That's what keeps me out of a good deal of the gallery conversation, I suppose. I really don't have a close friend in here, now that Jerry's gone. Perhaps I'm not really looking for any.

Cell Study's where I do my rapping. In my cell I read or try to practice meditation. The latter is difficult, but I think I've made some progress.

The metaphysical aspects of yoga are really something else. Just about perfect for a place like this. But the physical end of it requires a highly individual type of discipline, the kind we are least prepared to accept as a premise for anything in this culture. We tend to think of our minds as somehow operating collectively, which is a total fallacy, as the Indian philosopher well knew four thousand years ago.

True discipline requires a yea-saying on the part of the individual which no outward authority can actually command. They may seem to, but positive behavior can never originate from reactive behavior. That is one reason so little good is ever done by people whose self-image

152

rests on the notion of being a member of society—which includes the vast majority.

But never mind. Hatha-yoga can be taken as physical therapy, and it seems to be helping my back. Really amazing. If I keep it up, maybe the chest, nose, and throat condition will improve. Worth a try, but I can't seem to give up smoking. The most pernicious habit of all. I can only try to keep it under control—first come the exercises in the morning, and I can hold out till after breakfast. That first smoke up in Cell Study really feels good.

Hedonist!

Sex is a sacrament, but who would believe it. Most people treat it as a dreadful chore. It's been glamorized too much, for one thing—treated as sort of a personality problem. Now people are doing ridiculous things, like groping around in the dark, trying to touch each other. Somebody's making money off it, you can bet.

Basically insane shit. To twit one's time away with words like this is the work of a fool. Idle Mind should be the name of this place.

But the snow is falling—the dread white stuff. Jim next door loves it, loves the cold and the snow, can't wait to get out in the yard. His last bit was in Auburn, where he worked in the prison library. He's well read, has worked his way through most of the classics. His own story reads something like Dickens. Broken home, orphanages, farms for boys, homosexual headmasters—the whole bit.

He has quite a hate on for the human race but manages most of the time to control it. He and Ralph have become fast friends. For a while I thought there was some kind of thing on between them, but that's just prison paranoia. I guess I'm jealous. Maybe it's good not to have your friends too close to you; you keep them longer that way. Harry's gone to Auburn, as have most of the guys from Syracuse I came up with. Auburn's out of the question, for me, now. There're rumors something's going to be jumping off there, anyway.

Riot rumors have cooled down since the summer. There are always those who are ready at any time for anything. Control of a population this size is no easy business. But they have the heavy stuff, the armaments, and in my estimation such action would be suicidal.

News of Jack Kerouac's death comes to me via Jim, who shoves his issue of *Rolling Stone* through the bars to me after evening lock-in. It really makes me sad. We met once, got drunk in the Village and stoned in Brooklyn Heights on some brutal black grass that looked like little pellets of rabbit crap.

A favorite word of Kerouac's, "crap." In 1962 he was still being besieged by legions of adolescent boys, urging him to come on with them for another turn at the road. They wouldn't leave him alone, they attacked his house out in Northport, L.I., and broke a door and a window. This was very disconcerting to Jack, as he was also going through marital troubles and just wanted some peace and quiet at home with his mother.

He never really got that far away from her in his ramblings, and it's not surprising many of his views became more or less conservative, critical of the direction youth was taking in this country, toward the end. He also couldn't stop drinking, and alcoholic outrage is never quite convincing.

The heck with all that, however. When *On the Road* came out, we had an alternative to the dry accusatory rasp of Joe McCarthy; perhaps it might be possible to really feel young again in this country. Many of my generation had already given up—sealed themselves in college libraries, fumbling with footnotes and yet one more paper on Henry James. Even their dissipations were lackluster, they had no style.

After the Korean War, the whole nation threatened to become the Peacetime Army. If it took the horror of Vietnam to awaken us to the fact that the average American is a militantly average American, and this is quite the way those in power would have it, then something is salvaged. The lockstep is at least temporarily broken, there are ripples in the ranks, there is Abbie Hoffman—

who really couldn't have existed without Jack Kerouac.

For Kerouac, for all his obvious childishness, gave back to us something that had been missing practically since Whitman: the poetry of experience. He invited you to share in the kind of feelings that project you toward the realm of action: Go out and look; see for yourself—respond to the challenge of finding beauty in it. Most important, *move,* do something.

Of course, the movement became a movement en masse, and that's just what killed it, or at least warped the central part of it into freakdom. The trips you take by yourself are the ones that count. Only the individual actually encounters experience. When the fraternity boys latched on, it was all over. Perhaps that's why Jack, in his late forties alcoholic doldrums, regressed, began cursing at them in bars from Lowell to Okefenokee. A sad spectacle.

A basically gentle man will do that. Pressed to the wall, he finds his intentions at cross-purposes with everything around him—the people he thought understood him most actually understand him least, and then it becomes hard to understand one's self—one drinks, begins flailing about clumsily, like a wounded bear.

The novel of experience is really poetry in disguise, and that is what Jack wrote. Maybe he wasn't the world's best or even America's greatest poet, but he had the soul, the instincts, of a poet, and if that conflicted with other parts of his personality, as it does in all of us, he at least showed us the amount of freedom to be obtained in refusing to let the conflict stifle us, in breaking free, in going out and seeing with our own eyes what's there, of digging the scene. Just when we were close to becoming a nation of voyeurs, via the narcotizing hypnosis of the media.

Of course, you can always end up in prison. But that's part of the risk. Jack, at least, was spared that. He was at heart just a good Catholic boy, very much attached to his mother, in love with his adopted country, and toward the end very much disturbed and perhaps secretly terrified by what was happening to the world around him.

We had a good evening, celebrating the sound of our voices. Bless you Jack, may you have found some peace.

Then there's Phil Roth and the question of the state of the soul of the Jew in modern America.

A sticky question, I don't suppose I really ought to venture into it—after all, it's not my problem. But I haven't met many writers in my life, not famous ones at least, and it seems unlikely I'll meet too many in here. I think we're still a bit ahead of Russia in that sense. We're not salting them away in jails and nut houses at quite the same rate. But then maybe we're destroying more in the bud, too—psychological wipe-outs at age fifteen.

Roth came to dinner at our house in the woods outside of Saratoga, an isolated spot called Lake Lonely. It really was, too. In the winter you could hear the ice creaking, booming and groaning, in the summer the crickets and mosquitoes—not much else. One of its main charms was the absence of police sirens. But the neighbors would be too close for Thoreau's liking.

Another story. Someday I'll write that one, but there's still too much pain connected with it. There's still too much love-gone-wrong, which is one of the hardest things to think about in here. You feel it, but you try not to think about it.

Roth was in the middle of a novel and a marriage breakup. Summering it at Yaddo, a place where downtrodden and nerve-racked writers could try to pick it up again, on grants. I never knew how one obtained a grant. I think the greatest mistake a writer can make is not going to Harvard for at least a year, or Princeton or Yale for a bit longer. Hell, it must have shattered Hemingway in those moments when he let himself examine the nature of his insecurity.

If you go to enough bars, sooner or later you're going to run into a Famous Writer. Saratoga had nothing to offer except bars, and of course the racetrack during the month of August.

Roth was sitting next to me in a back-of-town rathole clip joint favored by jockeys, pimps, and what-all, and I probably wouldn't have noticed him except for some reason, maybe because I was acting intelligent by keeping my mouth shut and drinking my beer, he started letting me in on a few ironic observations concerning the place and the nature of its clientele.

I was thoroughly down from the beating I was taking as an instructor in English at Skidmore College, where a clique of little old ladies, aided by some viciously trained harem eunuchs, were hell-bent on ringing back in the whole Victorian era, part and parcel. Every week was going to be my last, but I kept hanging on, slipping them *Steppenwolf, Siddhartha, Diary of a Madman, Journey to the End of Night,* Camus, *Notes From the Underground*—anything that might help shock this future generation of women out of their premature suburban split-level schizophrenia. I made enemies and they finally did me in, getting me branded as everything from an anarcho-syndicalist to a mainlining hophead sex pervert, and who knows but that's when the FBI first began bugging me, setting me up for a future Dangerous Person Dossier.

Who knows, who knows. Roth, playing the sardonic Jew, was convivial, so I invited him to dinner at Lake Lonely, just a short remove from Yaddo. He said he'd come, and the wife prepared the most fantastic spread of chicken cacciatore in her now-and-then inspired career. The mushroom sauce was something else.

We ate outside, the mosquitoes being in a temporary lull of activity, and later sipped wine in the living room while listening to an ancient recording of Lennie Tristano, rounding off the Italianate character of the afternoon and evening. I got hung up listening to Tristano, as usual, and forgot to make conversation. Anyway, I think he liked the cacciatore . . .

But now I'm just rambling. I shall lay my pen down and stand on my head for a few minutes. Then perhaps I shall go to supper. I don't know. I'm out of bread and Ralph's acting like he's angry at me again; I don't know whether to ask him for some.

I really feel for Ralph. To be forty, as sensitive as Holden Caulfield, and facing that much time in a place you absolutely despise, must be sheer hell. The best I can do for him is try to stay out of the conversation. He blew up at me the other day, and I thought there was going to be trouble.

But we got past it.

Son of Man, Child of the Universe. What I understand you to mean is this: By loving you, I am loving mankind. For all the thoughts of man have been embraced by your consciousness, and there is no dark secret of the human heart you haven't seen. Transcending this, you became the Son of God.

But history is simultaneous when such a state of mind is present, and so it is correctly written that it was written. Prophecies of the future are also descriptions of the past. Caesar is still crossing the Rubicon, Christ is still being crucified, and maybe we will one day wake up to the fact of the Resurrection. I think that's exactly what the mind of man wishes to resist the most. The idea that he can't really bury his mistakes but must live past them.

We are buried here, O gentle Jesus, but we will be heard of—I feel it in my bones. Just how it will happen, I don't know, but I feel it in my bones. And I've had visions. These latter make me scared—I'm afraid of bloodshed.

Violence is a fact of life, a fact of birth, a cliché, a truth. But it stands apart from no other truth. How to live with it requires a recognition of the rest. We can't all be Gandhi, and even Gandhi's nonviolence had its violent aspects. To want to change anything in the world is to wish to do some form of violence to it. When we walk across the beach, we are upsetting molecules, perhaps destroying worlds. Tread softly, stranger. The turf you tread on may contain a universe or two.

However, tread we must. And so he came, and taught

us to wear sandals or go barefoot. Sometimes the lesson didn't go down.

Sometimes it's considered a form of paralysis. But Jesus walked, knowing wherever he went, worlds would be upset. The Father would forgive because he wasn't doing it willfully. He was only obeying the command of his nature, and in that there was an identity with the Father. There was harmony and no destruction that was not meant to be.

All others are an illusion. God is Love, and love destroys nothing except to replace it again with something better. But it can only do this, here on earth, here below, as a matter of conscious choice. Hence the Son of Man let everything rest on the individual.

It was bold and much too daring. The myth of history had to be perpetrated, and to do so would take a conspiracy of all those who were opposed to the idea. Which is why history is a graveyard and why there are prisons for those who try to wander outside its bounds.

For the love of God.

There is a sadness in love which nothing can hide, not even the brightest smile. Without love there is nothing really to care about. Life is simpler that way, and most people would prefer it, or so they think, so they have been taught to think. But they have been taught, generally, by all the failures of the world. And the greatest failure there is comes when one rejects love as a meaningful proposition.

Love is so hard to control. When we violate it by rejecting the reality of our feelings, it's a sure sign that we've gotten out of control. Because in the end, we control nothing. We only recognize what's there and work with it, and if it won't yield to our ideas of reason, we'd better change some of those ideas.

The Sufis understood that love was a form of madness; they considered it divine instead of merely pathological. Erich Fromm aside, the average psychiatrist is intent on proving the latter. And he's backed by everybody from the President on down. Dr. Skinner has become the spokesman of the American psychological establishment. His job is trying to convince us that a white rat really doesn't have it so bad.

Evidently, some still need convincing. It's amazing. Two world wars, Korea, and Vietnam somehow haven't managed to kill off all the artists among us.

ᒥᒐᒥᒐᒥᒐᒥ

The wild night contains a thousand terrors. Why this wake-up time, when everything is quiet?

Except the howling of the wind. Maybe that was it —the wind was full of voices, old dead voices, sharp new voices, babies crying, and the screaming of mothers.

Roll up a Bugler, light it, and try to stop shaking. Only it's Cayuga—state-cultivated horseshit. If your stomach can take it, it's all right.

Why write this. My hands are shaking, it's cold, the hack cracked all the dorm windows wide at 2 A.M., even though it's blowing and snowing, the son of a bitch.

Ralph likes the cold, he says. He got a wrench and fixed the end window so it won't really close. Fresh air is good for you, he says.

I think he's right, or I'd move my cell—it's warm on the other end of the gallery, where the snuggle-bunnies all seem quite satisfied.

Heat can be just as debilitating. As soon as the hack goes round again, I'll run through my yoga exercises. My hands feel as cold as those of a corpse, but I can't stop shaking.

Generally, sleep is no problem. But on nights like this it's as though something were trying to remind you how it felt to be really alive. What a waste your bones are going to, what a trap your mind has fallen into . . .

I can hardly see enough to write. I'll write anyway, hoping my mind will see what's necessary, getting some of it down.

This could happen to anybody, I'm convinced.

Temptation is just a stone's throw away from opportunity. And in a society where the government habitually commits crimes, crime seems irrelevant, unreal, entirely relative to the position the individual feels himself in, how much he thinks he can get away with.

I'm convinced you can get away with nothing, in the long run. Not me, not even Rockefeller. Money gives you a respite, but eventually you'll have to pay for that illusion. All illusions have to be paid for, and the price becomes higher the longer you can force situations that will sustain it.

Power. Power to the people. But the people have the power already; they merely suffer because their illusions are enforced by those who most recognize the power of greed: the greedy rich or those who aspire to be.

We all do. We'll keep voting for millionaires so long as they continue to represent the archetypes, the source of dream-stuff, all our secret aspirations.

Unlimited power, that's what we crave. The ability to become some kind of god on earth. The habitual petit-larcenist knows this feeling, although habit may have replaced original motivation.

Psychological theories of crime are cute, but it all starts with a need for the chemical reaction that takes place in some original confrontation with choice. The earlier the confrontation occurs, the less distinct the choice is apt to be. By the time a child starts to walk, he has some intimation as to just how far he will go. After that, it's a question of whether he can respect who's guiding him.

Respect is a unique combination of fear and love. Almost a balance, but love has the edge because it's been forced to a greater recognition: that the object it fears may be also the object it loves.

I was willing to dream, bleed, risk, and sacrifice, but I wasn't willing to be thought a fool. Which is probably why I'm here, in a Fool's Paradise.

Vanity is the source of just about everything that goes on in the human scene, as Ecclesiastes observed.

I wanted to experience life more than anybody else because I thought I could, because I thought somehow I was uniquely fitted for that.

But this is life, too . . .

Well, this is Thanksgiving.

And then you might ask, "Oh, Jesus, God, why did you make it so beautiful if your only object was to torture us into the recognition of its true beauty?"

You might ask that and never get an answer. Then again, somebody, a child, might just whisper the answer into your ear.

The problem is in keeping the ears open. So much static has filled them, so much wax, so much pollution. The sense of smell is fairly easy to give up on, but when the ears no longer receive any message, blindness cannot be far away.

Last night I heard a concerto, I think it was Beethoven's Second Piano, Serkin at the keyboard. My life has been so caught up in the rhythms of jazz I had almost forgotten this kind of pause—a structured search into the interior of the mind. Too many people had lied to me about the consequences of doing otherwise.

They're devastating, but so is life—and isn't that what we're all looking for, especially now, when death is such a suffocating commonplace? And the rationalist architects of history haven't been able to do a single thing to alter that fact. Whatever they start out to do, they end up demonstrating it.

Please forgive me. These words slip out, but I can't keep them going. It's too cold in here, I'm too tired.

DECEMBER

Up in Cell Study, it's becoming a menagerie. I don't know whether I'm influencing anyone or not, but they're giving me lots of latitude, and I feel as though I've made a few points.

Nobody really runs the scene. Periodically Mr. G., the new registrar, tries, but he knows his voice is getting fainter.

Even Diz keeps himself absent most of the time. He claims he's looking for a softer setup over in E-Block. I won't say I'm sorry to see him leave, but it's really a better place for him. There's a lot more hustling to be done under the merit-token system. In E-Block they pay you for doing things to help yourself, like taking courses in Cell Study. So the cons come up and dicker with the instructors. None of them dicker with me, though. They know I'll either give them an A or drop them, depending on whether or not they give me anything worth looking at.

Some of them really want to learn something in here, and that's about the only thing that keeps me going. Signs of intelligence gleam out from the most unlikely rathole corners. Once in a while you meet somebody who should have been a genius.

Word gets around. I've got people coming at me from all blocks, black, white, and Puerto Rican—I can't do a thing for them and they know it, but they like to rap. Many of them believe that education is a good thing. I tell them that the only education is self-education and suggest books to read.

The library is both puny and bureaucratic. I dig the guy who runs it, but only because he manages to temper his hatred of whites with a certain idea of what it takes to be a man.

He's a man, too—forget the Zulu stuff. He promotes black interests all over the prison, paints pictures that sell at outside local art shows, leather crafts, woodworks, and runs a tight ship in the library. He has more than ten years in and is working hard at making parole next time around, in a year or so. A politician, a diplomat, a leader. But there's a tide coming up under him which even he won't be able to withstand. The young blacks are filtering in, and their main characteristic is a complete loss of patience. Wild-eyed and irrational as many of them may be, there are also the cold silent calculators, and the intelligence level is rising perceptibly.

Maybe it just seems that way, maybe mine is diminishing. I'm getting some better students now, ones who would really like to get something out of the courses. I've got a creative-writing thing going, of sorts. Call three or four of them up at the same time and we sit around and jaw, sometimes about writing.

It's a drag, but also a test of memory and a relief from boredom. To be able to cail your shots this way gives you a slight feeling of freedom.

Freedom of assembly. Officer O'Sullivan doesn't like it but there's not much he can do as long as the doctor is in control. The doctor is leaving soon, pushed upstairs to the ecclesiastical heaven of the pulpit.

Would you believe? Protestant services, which means he doesn't have to be at the joint five times a week and then some. It's definitely a move up, and the divinity degree held him in good stead, after all.

They say a black man is taking over Cell Study. Good for him—somebody ought to take it over. It's really getting out of hand . . . The other day there was a lineup in the john for blowjobs. Some guys are just taking advantage. The doctor wasn't there and a new hack was on. He didn't seem to notice a thing. I beat it back to my desk and waited for the roof to fall in, but nothing happened.

Which is also a main feature of this joint.

Eight months. Technically, I'm a short-timer, having served half my bit. But it seems like a sea of days is still ahead of me, and I can't quite get the hang of placing my mind in the future.

Everything seems slowed down in the winter. One cold after another, but they seem a little less severe, last perhaps a little less long. I still think about death a lot —which is a form of death—and the idea of parole doesn't appeal to me a bit. But it's great to be half alive.

The new civilian in charge of Cell Study is the Reverend Lewis P. Richards, a right smart gentleman who, given a proper set of directions, might even get his shoes tied.

Actually, he's probably a genius in disguise. But he's been disguised so long, it's hard to know. It only took him one week to upset everything completely.

Black *esprit,* of course, is increased by having him up there. But it's really laughable.

Diz is talking of moving to E-Block again. He's laid off me for the past three months, which I think has only added to his keen sense of frustration. He's really getting nowhere as a Leader in Institutional Life. His militant rap is not quite as interspersed with "rednecks" as it used to be—the new registrar doesn't dig him at all and he knows it.

Mr. G. has almost ten years in on a rape rap, and it's already driving him batty about making parole. He doesn't like Flip mouthing off the way he does, which is constantly.

He doesn't like me, either. Which is a drag to find

out after I told him to move into the vacated cell next to me. According to him, I'm some kind of radical fruit-cake. We walked the yard one day and I had just swallowed an A Train and it was quite a scene. Everybody in the yard dug it—Mr. G. was close to being Mr. Attica in some ways. Nothing much happened in the joint that he didn't know about first.

"Coons, you're one of those secret militants," he started in. "I've been watching you, baby."

"What do you mean, secret?"

"I mean, they ain't figured you guys out yet."

Of course, there had to be a secret conspiracy, there couldn't only be just one me. That thought would make him even more nervous. But I let it go.

Mr. G. can't figure out why I rap so well with the other brothers. Most of my students are black, and after the initial interview either we get along fine or they decide not to take the course. Once in a while an ass-hole slips by, but you can't win them all.

My main idea was to make my job as easy as possible. Therefore I didn't do business with the E-Block people, who were doing their bits under a merit-system program and could offer you handy bribes for a fixed course, and by this means were compiling the best of possible parole-review records. I had to squash that shit at the outset, because once you bite you'll get more than you can swallow. Also, I really tried to do a few things with the courses on occasion, and if you corrupt your own system, you have only yourself to blame. I'll pass a man on appearance or if he really thinks he needs such bullshit on his record. But he at least has to show me a better rap than the average asshole who comes up to my desk. And the guys who really want to learn something, I'll help. The amount of effort it takes is often just enough to keep my mind halfway straight. Some of these bastards would make you cry . . .

Mr. G. scowls, showing his fortyish features in full

relief as we round the TV corner and head down weight-lifter's alley.

"I know you got something up your sleeve," he says.

"Other than my arm?"

"Don't kid me, baby. I know you're a militant. What do you plan to do about it?"

"Shovel their shit right back to their doorsteps. What's your idea?"

"I don't know, man. But this joint's going to *blow,* you know that."

"Yeah, but I don't like to think about it."

"Man, I'm telling you, Coons—this is serious business. They're loosening up a bit right now, but they'll tighten it again, wait and see. It's their old game, I've seen it. When this place blows . . ."

There was nothing to say. Mr. G. is right. They've loosened some of the springs, and the machine seems to be floundering a bit. Some of the pettier rules have gone off the book or are simply being ignored. B-Block went on strike, closing down the machine shop more or less for a week. As a result of which, they had to give us some of the raises that were already scheduled. The guys who got screwed worse in the deal were—guess who?—B-Block.

The main idea was to avoid what happened at Auburn, where they rioted along racial lines. This wasn't a race thing; they just wanted better wages. Also, some kind of safety rules and equipment. And insurance against all those missing fingers.

They got a five-cent raise. The school did a lot better. Instead of a dime a day, I'm now getting fifty cents.

Maybe I'm worth it. I can forget the despair when I'm rapping with other convicts. Up in Cell Study the day goes fairly fast. A few interviews, a quick trip through the morning's lesson envelopes, a cup of coffee, a trip to the john to wash your underclothes or perhaps shave, more coffee, more rapping. Waiting for the bell, marching back to D-Block, locking into your cells, waiting for the hack to take his count, lining up for chow, marching through the tunnels to the main mess hall, waiting in the serving line, eating, marching back through the tunnels to D-Block, waiting, marching, waiting.

Time goes fastest when you're rapping, so you keep doing that. It gets to be a habit, and there's always someone to look forward to seeing. Chink from B-Block, a Negro machinist who's into spiritual metaphysics and J. Krishnamurti; John, a Bronx Jewish kid who works at the warden's house and runs all over the institution; Humphrey, a graying Nordic blond who's writing a book about all the broads he screwed during his days as an electric appliance repairman. Others. Always a new face, sometimes a sign of intelligence, and from there you can get into just about any kind of conversation you want.

"Hey, man, what do you think of this guy Mailer?" Chink says, sitting down at my desk.

"A genius, but I wouldn't want him to marry my sister," I say, and we're off.

If it weren't for a few right dudes in here, this place would be sheer murder. Instead of just a matter of killing time . . .

Drugs in prison are a bore, so I mostly leave them alone. But the pall of Christmas is coming upon us, and I could almost go for something that would bind my mind up and keep it away from certain heavy thoughts.

About all they have here are downers. A Trains and the like. My tendencies toward depression don't need any further help.

I've plowed through Dostoyevski's *The Idiot*. All he does is remind me how hysterical we all are. It's a wonder the Russians haven't all turned into dope fiends. But they're basically a bunch of farmers and prefer to get twisted from a bottle.

Chink is for the Revolution in Consciousness. I am, too, but now we've got a real radical in our ranks, a guy named Sam Melville—Harry's Mad Bomber. They gave him the algebra desk across the room, and he's kept a quiet lip the first few days, but I can see he'd like to rap. He was downright offended by some things Chink and I were saying to each other.

"There can *be* no real revolution except inside the individual," Chink was saying. "All others are bound to fail, have always been doomed to failure. Systems themselves are doomed to failure; they must fail—it's their nature to fail."

Melville was passing by and paused to give us a scowl. He has a good scowl, just right for a Mad Bomber —which is a cutting thing to say. But everyone carves out his own psychic territory in prison, and up in Cell Study we were all individuals, no matter how tatterdemalion. Don't Tread on Me, Brother . . .

I won't tread on him, possibly because he's a big guy,

over six feet, lanky, loose-limbed, and a full set of calluses on his knuckles from practicing karate against brick and stone jailhouse walls. A heavy dude, this one. And very much alone, I would guess.

Just a little piece of the action, that's all that's wanted. A chance to put it into the next guy before he does it to you. Revolutionary raps are one thing, what a person does in the streets is another. The cutthroat philosophy prevails here, and if it's a historical anachronism soon to be swept aside, Sam's going to need an awfully big broom.

What is a prison but a reflection of the general power structure? Status conferral, pecking orders, organized hustles—these are the things that preoccupy the average mind—and what else could you expect? The system breeds criminals because it needs criminals. How else are we going to know who's respectable and who isn't? Besides, a criminal produces capital. He provides jobs for law-enforcement agencies, lawyers, courts, judges, correctional officials. He moves goods, creates markets—look at all the locks that have been sold in the last few years. He has learned to exploit, but he is also exploitable.

The locker industry here grosses something like five million a year. The lockers are supposed to go only to other state facilities, hospitals and the like, but many arrive by indirect routes at other profitable destinations. The commissary is a rake-off, an outside distributor has a lock on the business and milks it for all it's worth. He has to grease the machine, too, so nobody complains except the convicts.

They complain, anyway, because there's too much time, too much monotony, too much boredom. A good number of them would run this prison even more ruthlessly than the present authorities. "Bring back the chair!" you can almost hear some of them saying. They have very low opinions of human nature.

The lowest. They're convinced nobody's really much better than themselves.

ⅢⅢⅢ

Why should anyone do anything for a convict? He's lower than a snake; we all know it. He has the morals of an alley cat, the conscience of a coyote. He'd murder his mother for a dime and use it to call his pusher. Hadn't we better send such human vermin to the exterminator?

Why not, except his poisonous ashes might do more to pollute the atmosphere, even more than Detroit, Du Pont, and U.S. Steel combined. Throw in the Atomic Energy Commission and B. F. Goodrich if you like—there's nothing worse than convict shit. It should be buried, perhaps, in sealed containers deep beneath the salt mines of some central-western state. It should never again see the light of day.

Let us wash our hands of it. But then, of course, we must be willing to pay the price. The price of clean hands is often dirty linen. It's hanging out now even in the tidiest suburb, and if you can't quite see it flapping in the breeze the way you can from downtown backyard tenements, it's because the Laundromats have the business and almost anyone can manage to afford an automatic dryer. But there's phosphates in the detergent, and a lot of the streams are completely polluted. Even mother's milk shows strong traces of strontium 90.

Not to imply there's any kind of critical situation. We've gotten along like this for years; prove to me there's no tomorrow. Meanwhile the tide keeps rising, and there are those who claim a benevolent dictatorship is the answer, the only solution. People can't be responsible for themselves; that whole idea went down the drain, along with Thoreau, Emerson, and all those crusty people. It's actually bad to have people think they can be responsible for themselves, since then they get other strange notions, too—like self-government.

Who really wants it? There are bells to wake us up in the morning and officers to remind us the nighttime is for sleeping. There are freeways, and we soon won't even have to touch the damn steering wheel to drive to work.

On the other side of Disneyland there's a prison. Mickey Mouse is the warden, and his hands circumnavigate the sphere of time itself, pointing always to the fact that time is wasting. The Captain of the Guards walks with a waddle and quacks like Donald Duck. He's had years of experience in the barnyard and knows how to handle these critters. If they don't move the way you tell 'em, use the stick.

That's All, Folks!

Really a depressing day.

"How you want it, man?"

"Not really short, but, you know—even, neat-like."

"Gotcha."

The barber shop is on the top floor of some building in the interior; it has windows and looks out over a vista that might temporarily have satisfied the soul of the unsettled pioneer.

"A little valley," he might have said. "I could settle down here if I had me a woman . . ."

Treacherous thoughts, ones that bogged down our ancestors in many a quagmire. Better he should have kept on going, trying to prove once and for all the earth is flat.

The barber is cool. He could shave my head or slit my throat, but what he's really interested in is learning the profession. If a guy came out of here without knowing something useful, it was his own fault.

This whitey had vibes, and besides, someday he might be a good tipper. There was really nothing to taking a head: one quick motion and it was all over. That gave you a certain feeling of power. But power kept under control might earn interest. And this whitey, he had kind of a crazy gleam in his eyes. Like he didn't give a fuck what you did, he was *there* already . . .

Naw, impossible. But on the other hand you never knew. Strange things were taking place. The Brothers were starting to talk to Whitey on a slightly different level. Like maybe they might capitalize the letter W. Some token sign of respect.

They'd turned that school upside down. Man, this was one of the motherfuckers!

But he looks old. He ain't no kid, this one. But he looks young, too. Middle-aged? Yeah, that's about it. Only not average middle-aged, because now he was staring out the window and looked at least a thousand years old.

Man, can that bullshit. This dude's been to the other side, that's all. I bet if I pulled my dick out on him, he'd just laugh.

Ha-ha! Out of sight!

"How's that look?"

"Really peculiar. Like I almost forgot I was in prison, for a moment."

"Yeah? Which one was that?"

"Well, you see that cloud out there?"

"That's a cloud, man."

"Yeah. Maybe that's why it looks so free."

"You got a point. Later, man."

"Later."

Then it's lineup for back to D-Block.

The tunnels are colored gray, but not by a very good artist. The arched windows as you passed them offered vistas, marvelous vistas of prison yards. A prison yard looks just like the kind of place you'd need if you wanted to keep penned-up people in clear gunsight. Open, barren.

Add bleak to get winter. A prison yard is always wintry, even in the grass-burn heat of midsummer. But it is seldom as barren as it is in winter.

In winter it is really barren, and also bleak.

Fuck Hemingway. The yard is a runnel of tunnels, carved in the snow by mad housewives, consecrated to the proposition that there is deviation, even in straight lines and even some in curves. It used to be a man trapped in the wrong tunnel would have to give up something, probably his most prized possession. In many cases this was his ass. It was not the rule, even though some people still persist in believing so.

So Ralph is really a victim of service in the Marines. If I didn't know that, one of us might have killed each other sometime. Gradually, as he raps to Jim in the next cell at night, I learn his whole story.

It sums up pretty easy: A sensitive and alcohol-prone kid from a decaying middle-class scene joins up with the Marines in order to face the question of his manhood. The battlefield just about intoxicates him, when he's not vomiting. Which gets to be about as often as the next guy.

Chapter Two: Ralph decides fuck the question of his manhood, it faded one night in a mid-Pacific shanty-bar and hasn't really come up since. So fuck that and fuck this war. Get me out of here.

Ensuing chapters: After this decision, Ralph has to learn what death is like by almost getting his nuts blown off. It puts him away long enough to come home a hero, and then of course there's the GI Bill and a small college down in Virginia . . .

That really made you want to puke. After what he'd seen, how could the professors say such things? How could they even dare to get up there and *say* them?

So it was arguments with professors, and drinking. Drinking was a favorite sport among the veterans, so at first he was hardly noticed. But outright anonymity wasn't his forte, either. He had developed a habit of finding himself next to marines or ex-marines and kind of fucking them over about the war.

"If they hadn't dropped the bomb, we'd never have beaten them."

"Beaten who? Look, soldier; the Marines were at the *doors.*"

"Fuck you, I was in the Marines and I know better."

His wounds only deepened, and first it was petty thievery to pay the bar bills and then it became go-for-broke.

But Ralph's story is Ralph's story—what right have I to it? What he really wants to do is write it himself. I hope someday he does, it's so next to a lot of us.

These kinds of thoughts pursue you as you wait in line for a move-up toward the doctor's window. Then you faint, because the thought hits you you really don't know what this is all about . . .

"I can't get any reading on his blood pressure."

"See if he can walk. Take him to the hospital."

It could have been a thought. A thought that had been growing since they delivered the forwarded telegram from my sister about someone dying in a state mental institution.

But I knew it already. I knew she was dying from the letter I got in County Jail, the one that said "we." They'd broken her spirit in some final way, forcing her to be pure in heart. But she always had the heart of a child.

Then there were those feelings that wake you in the middle of the night and tell you things more explicit than telegrams. I didn't know she was dying, I knew she was already dead.

Funeral

The landscape is sullen under almost-spring skies. It would be leaden except for cracks of light between the clouds. The hills look brown and moist, ready to accept more snow if they have to. The trees stretch upward.

The car is colored dark, the officers wear sports coats. The handcuffs are loose, the back seat is comfortable. The waist chain bites a bit, and I lean forward, clinking the link chain from the waist chain to the handcuffs. The detective on the right glances over his shoulder.

"Everything okay?"

"Everything's fine."

It really feels good to be on an outing like this—if I had a notebook, I'd write down just how good it feels. Three-hundred-some-odd miles of chains and handcuffs. Nice. Perhaps in a few small towns they'd parade me down Main Street: Dangerous Person On Display—See How Acid Freaks Look After We Get Through With Them! Cops will do anything for a buck.

Meanwhile there was the New York State Thruway scenery to be contemplated, enjoyed if possible. It hadn't changed much, but you still had to be amazed at the variety of types of trees along the way.

Let the mind go numb, become a receptacle. Keep it light and tragicomic. The State of New York was going to considerable expense to take you to this funeral—was there any way you could fail to show gratitude?

And after all, what was all the fuss about? What was she to you? A figure who tore you to pieces once, but by now it should have been healed.

Was it? Why didn't you write?

Your Honor, I thought I'd be out of this place in time to go see her. She wasn't that old.

"You had plenty of time to do that before, didn't you, son?"

"But I never really knew her. I never knew who she was, this strange woman who used to come stay at our house when I was a child—"

"I don't want to hear any more of this! I'll give you the lightest sentence I can, but you better do every day of it!"

"Thank you, your Honor. I promise not to come back with a gun and shoot you."

"Three years! For your own benefit, of course—in Attica State Prison. You can get psychiatric therapy there once a week and— Next Case!"

Thank you, your Honor, thank you, your Honor.

"A broken home seems to be the source of the problem here," Mr. Jones says sadly, tapping the open folder before him on the desk with his pink and neatly manicured forefinger.

I nod solemnly. It's the worst kind of insult but one he can't legitimately refuse. You're supposed to argue with him, to let him get his teeth in the jugular of your weakness. That's his job—always to point to your weakness. To show you why you have failed as a Man.

He looks at me, momentarily flustered, but only a quick blink of his steel-blue eyes gives any indication of that. He takes his pencil in one hand and taps it between the thumb and forefinger of the other. He smiles, and it would almost be hideous except for the Benevolent Directness of the smile. All his dentures are in order. His brush cut is military, his flesh pinkly scrubbed.

His house in a nearby township is recently painted. White. His degree from Cornell I.L. & R. is framed above the mantelpiece, intact for the foreseeable ages.

It's a goddamned shame that I went to Cornell, too, but there's nothing he can do about it. Some stupid shithead this must be—getting himself framed up like that. Two years of teaching, it's embarrassing. But private information tells us he's a sex pervert as well as a drug addict. They got him out of the teaching game, but why the hell do I have to handle him now? Christ, why don't they just *shoot* them . . .

"I'd say it was a problem," I say after my solemn nod. And all the rest of what I was going to say is lost as I begin to stare vacantly at his unplugged tape recorder.

What a bunch of shit. This guy never did anything off the record in his life, let alone forget to tape an interview. But he's had a course in psychology as an undergrad, and he's figured it out that if I see the unplugged plug on his desk, I'll loosen up enough to at least make some interesting conversation. Meanwhile there could be six tape recorders grinding away behind his desk. Fuck him—if he wants anything from me, he'll have to invite me out to a bar for a drink, and that's that.

A shame, but I can't do anything more for him. And he can't do a thing for me, and he knows it, and that's what grates him. So he'll forget that business about my sex life, at least for this interview. Just as long as I remain polite . . .

You think I don't see you. But I never had a dream that didn't include you. You think I don't hear you. But your music kept me falling for the girls who couldn't be mine.

Don't tell me, black man, to pay my dues. My old man never owned slaves, nor his. They came for a piece of land, and they sometimes married with the Indian natives. But they bought more than they stole, and they killed less than anybody after them.

The killers came later, wearing blood on their coats.

But nobody's out to teach you White History. It sucks, the same as yours. For every brag it makes, you can count the corpses. The sons went wrong, the daughters became ignorantly promiscuous, the parents took to drink and gambling. It's an old story, and it's yours as well as mine.

Somewhere in this country there's a thread they still haven't broken. I think the best thing we can do now is try to find it, you and me.

Standing in a bar on lower Sixth Avenue, my head tripping out like crazy, and this voice comes to me: "Come on, baby, light my fire!"

His name Feliciano, a blind Puerto Rican. The voice, the guitar, was where everything was at. It impinged, penetrated, mixed itself into the bloodstream and took the mind to a place where warmth and romance were synonymous. Total intoxication with the thought of a certain chick, that's what it was.

She wasn't real, of course—merely a persistent hallucination, one that came up every time I tripped. And most of the time that I didn't. I defied the acid to melt and corrode the sensation of her milk-warm flesh against my gently sliding lips, but it couldn't. It could only show me how deep within the layers of myself the impression had gone. All the way down to the subterranean vaults, and there are still parts of this dungeon I must walk through. There is somehow love here, too.

But it's so hard to believe.

Usually it's like chasing after shadows. However, now and then you see it—just a glimpse. And that's amazing.

But I can't sustain it. I'm too tired and my lungs are too full of this winter, this tacky, sticky, damp, and dingy winter. It settles in my chest, making my body a constant battleground, my mind a slightly out-of-focus camera lens, trying in vain to catch a thought that isn't fleeting. Maybe I'll go back to writing song lyrics again. Prison songs ought to be getting large pretty soon. There's a lot more kids in here than there ever used to be. There's Bobbie, who plays a pretty decent rock guitar. Never had much more than a nickel's worth of grass, so they busted him for that, on another trumped-up sale: nine years.

He'd do maybe eighteen months if he didn't fuck up, but then he'd have the parole thing hanging over him till he was thirty. Wife and one kid.

Then there's Billy, also twenty-one, also married, also no previous offense, also in on a grass bust. Some ex-girlfriend informed on him, and six months later an indictment came down. For giving away a nickel bag, he drew zip-seven. Seven years a ward of the state. But he could handle it, he was young and he had religion. Also enough brains to be writing his own writs. Sings in the choir on Sundays, too. Just a bright-faced kid some asshole hick judge decided to make an example of.

Let them keep on. They're driving the kids into heroin, and maybe that's just what they want. More profits at the top. You can't make the big dollar on grass, which is why the Mafia tried to squash it, even lending paid informers to the police. They hated to see the kids getting high on stuff anyone could grow in their backyard. As things stand now, many "agents" are getting their pay both ways.

So we'll turn the nation's youth on to real hard-core junk. Then we'll set up an Addiction Control Agency, and maybe we can make some money out of that. But keep these free-lancers off the street—they're a bug to corporate enterprise!

Also, grass is subversive. It makes people stop and think about their thoughts, and we can't have that. Ask Dr. Skinner. He's an expert on White Rats. He's stuck electrodes up their ass and taken their temperature and even sniffed the results with his delicately conditioned nose. He's familiar with the Source of White Ratshit. Intimate, you might say. What's good for white rats is good for the country.

O Lord, deliver us from the Behaviorists!

In the name of everything sacred.

"The only thing to do with a cold is go lie down."

"Yeah, but you get sick of that. What I need is a fifth of Rémy Martin and a bitch."

"What we all need, brother. That's all out there."

"Yeah. I don't care for the ones in here."

"They don't look so bad after you've been here long enough."

"Sure, but who wants to stay that long."

"It's not so bad with the short bits. A chance to get yourself together."

"I'm hip. But you got to do it yourself. They aren't really offering you anything."

"Well, you got to have your *own* program, you dig?"

"Yeah. But I'm having trouble getting mine together. It's like I know what I *should* do, but I can't get around to making the moves."

"Well, you got to start with one. You can lay up in your crib and see the whole thing pass before your eyes, but if you don't get one foot on the floor, it won't be anything but an old movie."

"Dig it, brother—I dig the way you rap. What you got for me up there in Cell Study?"

"A whore, a Cadillac, and a bottle of gin."

"Bullshit. You ain't talkin' to no square-ass nigger, I done had me those things. Whatcha *got,* man?"

"English, mostly."

"What good is it?"

"Teach you to put the right words in the right pockets, which is like a step or two above pocket pool, you dig?"

"Man, you're a motherfucker. What else you got?"

. . . I thought, wondering for a moment if he was under the impression he was about to put a foot in the door of the Big Time Drug Circuit, if he really knew that I had once been on the verge of cornering the entire Northeast, that in my navy pin-stripe and flowing red beard, working my way down the flagstone of a brilliantly lit autumn campus landscape, a casual grasp on the solid gold head of my antique mahogany walking stick, I would gather the eyes of loving greedy clods and co-eds who heretofore had only known the professor by reputation, which had spread like wildfire that flaming season of the acid-etched Vermont and Massachusetts woods.

No, how could he know any of this. Of the campus dance floor, the girls in mini-dresses, and the rock band revved on *Leaves of Grass*. Vibrations reached us from the center of the earth; the room trembled as our feet struck sparks against the floor. And how I frightened you and felt sorry afterward, wondering if I should have left you alone or even frightened you some more—

"History. American History with World Backgrounds, or World History with American Backgrounds, depending on how far you need it twisted."
"That all?"
"Astrology and the Art of Cosmic Rape."
"That sounds good. I'd like that one."
"Well, drop a tab to the school and bring your face."
"Solid! See you later, man!"

—or what we did in the woods that day, when the autumn fires were burning and the incense made our nostrils tremble slightly under blue skies and carnivals of branches reaching up for clouds made of cotton candy.

But I never showed up at the right time. I couldn't because our time was never right; it was the time of two

193

people who were looking for a world where they could be, and the dervishes might dance this way forever my love, but I still couldn't help it. The soft starlight of Saratoga woods and winter moons reflected itself from your eyes, and after many a season in moonless hell a man needs to hold a piece of that warmth. He needs to touch it, confirm its existence. He needs the benediction of such tenderness against his flesh, to lie down in the still waters of the night and find his hands hold more than emptiness, that the moon, the stars, are all there, that they are all very real, that this is not an alien or a deserted planet where life had struggled but ceased to exist.

If you'd ever wanted to be that, we could have made it. No other way.

The positive power of prayer is answered in the small miracles we most often take for granted. Observe: Diz has left Cell Study, and we never even laid a hand on each other. In a way I'll miss him. But not his aggravating ways.

In his place comes Hank, a soft-spoken, mild-mannered young man doing natural life. He'd been a member of a short-lived successful Harlem-based vocal group called the Moonglows. Success was something "Hanky" was ready to handle—but not the alcohol. Probably like me, he'd go through mean personality changes behind it, and in a fast scene that can be treacherous. Whoever he'd done in had probably been beside the point. That's the way it usually works out. Something that the next day would have been bullshit, only the whole thing went too far . . .

Melville's looking to get bounced from D-Block. I think he's frustrated here in his attempts to organize or combine with radical groups.

Sam's a swell guy. Give you the shirt off his back, but he won't wear the right one to the mess hall. His war on petty regulations has gotten him two keeplocks thus far, but each time the court dismissed them the next day. They're playing easy with him, maybe because of his outside lawyers, maybe just to see how far he wants to go.

What he wants to be is a hall porter in C-Block. My guess is they'll assign him to every other job in the place first. And they'll always give a reason why he couldn't get the one he wanted right then. After he's been through the blocks, they'll put him right back here. The school doesn't really want him either, but who else is qualified to handle so much mental power? You couldn't trust him alone in the halls; he might rewire the joint and blow it up. That would cause embarrassments when Albany came around.

So it's a war between the Weathermen and the Administration. It would be funny except nothing in this place stays funny too long. Sam's in trouble, but I don't know just what to say to him. We agree on ideological grounds only to the extent that Something Should Be Done.

"A Marxist revolution is the only answer."

"It hasn't been so far."

"China's come pretty far."

"Yeah, but it still needs old men to run it and periodic purges to keep it from suffocating. Who's kidding who? The Red Guards were kids getting sick of wise old men telling them every move. They were ready to listen, providing they could have their own harems and opium dens."

"That's slander against the Chinese leaders! How the hell can you say they've got opium dens!"

"Instinct. All the high-grade shit they've got over there has to be doing something for the economy. International dope deals can make a nation rich if it goes about it systematically. But you know as well as I do the dealer always takes off the top for himself. He's got to—it's a matter of prestige, if nothing else. And furthermore—"

"I don't want to hear any more of this shit. See you later."

So we're getting to be pretty good friends, only it makes me sad when I hear him playing the guitar down the gallery at night after supper.

Sad for all of us, I guess. Including the Chinese leaders.

Prison really expands your mind.

"But what are you *for?* It's easy to be against all these things, but what do you really want?"

Sooner or later they'll always put it to you like that —the sincere ones. Sam's sincerity impresses me but also scares me. Ideas are a dime a dozen—how far can a person commit himself to one or another? And he was probably thinking about me: How far can anyone with half a brain remain uncommitted?

Détente. What was happening was, he was beginning to feel sorry for me. He figured I'd grown old, jaded, from being fucked over too much by American Society, no doubt—which is a credit to his point of view, if anything.

But once you've seen through a bitch you've either got to have done with her or else try to give her a hand with the dishes now and then. Or whatever.

"Technological Democracy," I said.

Sam gave me the gimlets, his stubborn-set jaw loosening up into a semismile, his teeth showing, but just the lower ones. He gave the desk a light chop with the edge of his left hand—enough to suggest the sport was also a game of self-control.

"What's that?" he said.

"I think we should harness the advances of technology in certain fields—most specifically and immediately, electronics—to the end of creating a situation of genuine universal human suffrage. What I mean by that is, *everyone* votes, the only requirement being he or she is able to stand in front of a television set. They could hook it up that way—a continuous rating system, instantaneous response, the pulse of the nation having to say just what was most beneficial in regard to all matters concerning the nation's health . . ."

"Nationalism! That's sick, passé, simplistic."

That made me angry—he'd scored a point. I had allowed myself for an unguarded moment to take his question very seriously, to regard it on face value. *E Pluribus Unum,* it said!

Or in other words, Bullshit—a word they still won't print in *The New York Times.*

"Permitting the people to vote their own interest on every issue will provide the full definition of the national interest at any time. As for children voting, I've seen smarter two-year-olds than some of our leaders in Congress, and I'd trust my own kids with the bomb before I would any son of a bitch who's never—ah, forget it."

"I'm sorry. I'll see you in the yard."

Emotional intensity of argument becomes a bond of affection in prison. But I really can't Remember the War with dispassion, or with anything except the feeling of horror of having children in a world where nothing really counted after all.

I wonder how many people my age started in on a trip like that after J.F.K.'s assassination? What really scared me was, something I'd been writing at the time, in Cornell grad school, predicted it. But I think those pages are all thrown away, as my chairman was embarrassed to read them. There was a poem, too—all about the assassination, but I wrote them *before* it happened.

But then, of course, insanity can be explained in many ways.

Persistent as the teeth of smiling daisies, her image. Burned into the backside of my retinas, it gave me no chance to follow anything except the course of its duration. Strangely enough, this led me west, although she lay to the north and east—as though if I could find the source of the sunset, if I could rip the cords from their sockets and jam my thumb squarely in the electric eye of eternity, I would somehow short-circuit the machine that had programed me into this particular avenue of oblivion.

Lilah was her name. In years she was little more than a freshly burst blossom, petals still intact, decorated with pearls of virginal dew. But her eyes were ancient with wisdom. I loved her, but I fought it, and I won, and I lost.

By the time I knew that, I also knew I'd never see her again. Such knowledge is very hard to absorb.

He walks the yard and talks to the brothers. The Spanish brothers, especially, *mucho simpático.* Young Lords, they mean business. What is more, they often make sense. The animation they bring to the game makes up for all its shortcomings. They are not really culturally disadvantaged, just shit on. Their intuitions are intact, not warped and mangled by near-access to the thrones of greed. Their beat is steady; they maintain it during the motionless periods, when watching is the best thing to do. You can communicate with them, they are not afraid, they are not insular. Without hesitation they will call you Brother, and do not have to hear your political rap. They simply know you are with them or against, they have not lost the intelligence of the eyes.

Sam is trying to teach me Spanish, but I am one poor student. I want to learn it, but I don't want to look at words in books. I don't want to think about conjugations, verb endings. I want to hear the music, but I am really sick of words. I don't believe in them unless they are making music. It's as simple as that.

Joyce wrote poetry in her mind and sang it into my ear when she was six, waking me from some kind of deathly sleep, and I began again those thoughts that lead toward belief in angles wider than 360 degrees, sounds that look like color, pictures that make their own music, revealing the contours of a love that might have to go through a thousand transformations just to know the secret of one moment of being, just to taste for an instant its time-lessness.

The latinos make their own music, but they are aware of others.

"Somebody spoke, and I went into a dream."

"What's that?"

"A song, by the Beatles."

"Yeah, man—the Beatles."

"It's decadent."

"No, man—it's *about* decadence. There's a difference."

"They went commercial, didn't they?"

"No, they always were commercial. They merely exploited it."

"That's hip."

But Sam's annoyed because it isn't purist. Such thoughts can corrupt the revolution. But the revolution is among the corrupt and no place else.

How can I tell him this? To be pure, one has to defile himself and know he is defiling himself and that it is himself he is defiling. To be pure, one must eat the garbage of our civilization and say Yes to the life in it and No to the death in it. One never cheats death, but to cheat death-in-life is to recognize the game that is being played against us—the one that tells us all to go out and commit suicide, tonight . . .

So we will say Yes to them when we mean No; we will be their niggers as long as they need fantasies of niggers. For nothing else keeps them at all under control. A child who refuses to grow up is an old man dying of various conflicts which he would rather have result in cancer than relinquish. Pity our leaders, pray for them at night when there is nothing left to think of. Except your children.

Refrain from the possession of souls, but see if you can find your own. Don't worry about action, it will happen in its season. If not now, then later. Remember, there is no side to stand on—only the earth beneath your feet. Honeycombed with caves and subterranean river-flows and molten beds of lava, inundated with particles from the far-flung corners of the universe, it beats like a heart filled with the agonies of love for its most wayward children. Listen to it as it turns if you would be in tune with the force of revolution. And don't forget to smile as you greet the sun.

She's very pretty and likes to have it acknowledged.

JANUARY, 1971

It came down from Albany that we could have musical instruments, and for Christmas my sister sent me a tenor recorder. Really a strange instrument, but kind of nice once you get into it.

Mr. Sandman, the Nighthack, isn't even bothering with us tonight, so I take my trusty flute and whack out a few practice shots at "Auld Lang Syne." So far, it seems to have caused no major disturbance on the gallery. The first week or so it was touch and go, but now practically everybody's got something; Melville's guitar is blown away; he's over in A-Block or somewhere, mending fences with the tailor-shop girls, no doubt. Women of the Cloth, meet Weatherman. Wow!

Enough snides. Sam will handle himself wherever he is; his only problem is with the hacks. He doesn't really hate them much, but the system puts them directly in his way. Otherwise, they'd probably both be glad to ignore each other.

But being ignored by the hacks is considered a privilege in prison. And they're ignoring us tonight, which makes this a privileged gallery.

The inmates generally raise hell on New Year's Eve. Anything loose in their cells gets banged against the wall, often demolished; it's one big joyous celebration, just like in Times Square they're passing the bottle around—the hacks, that is.

The inmates have their own juice, home-manufactured. Donny the water boy got crocked early in the evening and laid himself right out on the gallery. Nicely polluted, and the hack didn't even come around to help him back in his cell for almost an hour. Out of sight, Donny . . .

The truce I have with Ralph in the last cell has broadened into something just short of friendship. Between us is Jim, who maintains relations both ways, but often with me only surreptitiously. He writes song lyrics, too, and we've passed samples back and forth. Some of his stuff makes me downright envious. Far-out, but controlled by a beautiful sense of rhythm and sound. Psychedelic beyond Dylan, only more Romantic. My stuff is bald by comparison, but he knows what I mean.

And so I find out Ralph writes poetry, too, and so does Hank, so we all decide to then and there have a reading.

It's a first—Ralph can't believe he's doing this. But what the hell, it's New Year's Eve. The rest of the blocks and galleries are going wild, ours is comparatively quiet. Donny hauled a cartful of goodies we'd chipped in for from the commissary earlier, and we supped on ice cream, cake, and nectar. The lights stay on till twelve or one, and talking's permitted. No hack making the rounds either—a half a dozen hacksaws would really embarrass this place tonight.

But Ralph was fresh out of blades, so we rapped poetry:

THE TRUMPETEER
In memory of Miles Davis, who still somehow lives

Alone in fragile balance
On the lip of morning murky coffee cups
Your blues began the day,
That magic might still come of all-night thoughts
And sleep could be pushed back before the city
Rose to haunt those dreams of where the heart
Could never hurt,
Could never beat with pity,
And wars could never wither breaks in time.
You sang in bubbled sound from sullen depths,
In purple prose-tones, sleepy with a lyric dash

And in the quavering almost-morning light
You sang where children once knew only fright,
Knowing the alone of 'Round Midnight.

Which isn't so bad if you consider the fact that some
of these dudes have been here since the fifties, when Miles
really had something to say. Before he started making
covers representing a black man's dream of Claire's knee.
Before he'd lost the poetry of Bop and found a way to
sing about the loss of poetry in Bop City, which was
nothing other than New York in pre-McCarthy fifties.

Before George Jackson, before they cut him down.

BEFORE

A cockroach walked across this page
As though to stop the thoughts that follow,
But I am not offended,
Only just enraged
Enough to write down anyway
What yesterday seemed hollow.

Unspeakably beautiful your lips,
Though they said next to nothing;
So deep the seaweed promise of your wide and almost
    open eyes,
I tried to fathom it with nets
And cables made of endless thoughts
Strung through years and miles to now,
Like bridges over nothingness,
Sad mountains in the evening of a passing train,
And children crying behind broken windows
For the food that had been promised
But somehow never came.

Glazed with tiny jewels your thighs,
Flowers that made my nostrils tremble

206

As my hand reached out to touch the meaning
Of roads that seemed forever,
Of roses painted on a wall,
Of stairways climbed and later on descended,
From years which had to pass before we met;
You were astonished as you leaned alone to look
Upon a world you'd never known
Before evening dressed in cardigan and snow,
And winter streets whose neon glow
Seemed etched in fires still burning low,
From before.

There was more, but everybody knows prison poetry
is stylized to the point of boredom and generally speaking a meretricious drag. Very little gets reviewed in the
Times.

There's not much to say about it. We're into 1971
now, the Year of the Board and perhaps my parole, or at
least conditional release. I should be quite happy. Some
of these people when they rap parole are talking about
the eighties. They have great confidence in our country,
despite everything that comes our way over the radio and
in the newspapers. Which is why I seldom rap politics—
I simply haven't the heart.

Now the lights go down, and some of us will sleep.
And some will test the power of prayer . . .

Today I got a visit.

It's all part of a plot to worry the authorities. What they like is cons who don't ever get any visits at all. That means they belong to the institution, and the institution is just as greedy as any other institution erected by an essentially greedy people. It likes to make sure a certain portion of its food is sacrosanct.

So I wrote my Old Man, whom the Bible has advised me not to call father, and just about told him what a son of a bitch I thought he really was.

Turned on the tears, too—and some of them were real. Mine or his, I don't know which. I don't know if a turnip sweats; I was never raised on a farm, like him. I never smelled of grease and motor oil and gasoline, like him, or breathed a heady aroma of pipe and cigar tobacco. Like him.

I guess I was never like him. It would have been nice to know it sooner, though. Which is about what I told him.

But I have to dig it. He never hit me, at that. Maybe it was only because he was never around long enough. Now he's seventy and willing to drive through three hundred miles of up-country winter snow and shit to come see me in prison.

There's nothing to be made up for, though. Nothing can make up for this; I've already written that idea off. What society has to offer, and it staggers the mind to think of it, can never repay a moment's loss of freedom

—once freedom has been recognized, known, accepted in all its liabilities and assets, farcical illusions and frenetic palpitations of a heart beating wild with the thought of love still possible, illusions to be tasted and teased into realities fecund with potential future.

My own seed has been sown; how can I forgive myself if I can't forgive him? So his answer was a surprise, and the call-out from Saturday afternoon Dale Carnegie session only half expected.

They send you to the Electric Gate with a pass, which the hack checks at Times Square, juncture of the above-ground tunnels which separate the Cloisters A, B, C, and D, and then it's into the strip room for a quick search of clothing, mouth, and asshole. They could at least let the chicks outside in the visiting room watch through a two-way mirror. It's a drag.

The visiting room is fairly large, lined with low counters topped with heavy-gauge chicken-wire fencing on three sides. You're supposed to remain seated while talking to Visitor. There will be no touching of hands, kissing, undue displays, etc. . . .

Well, I didn't really want to kiss my old man, anyway. But he looked pretty good, once I got used to the sight of a wispy-haired little old Santa Claus sitting there.

"I had a hell of a time getting here," he says, and proceeds to reveal some of the horrors of country roads in winter, just about the way they do while bragging around the gas station before closing. I really don't know what to say, but somehow I'm feeling good. This is like very real.

"I was going to bring you a hacksaw," he says. "But I couldn't find one."

"That's all right. You'd need more than a hacksaw for this place."

"Lots of bars, huh?"

"Yeah. Bring me an acetylene torch."

"Don't let the warden hear you saying things like that."

"He's deaf. How the hell are you?"

He's about the same as he was twenty years ago, only older. We may even go fishing when I get out.

Which is rather unbelievable.

FEBRUARY

Next week, the Board. A cold wind seems to whistle along the gallery for days after the Board has met. The vibes may have changed a little, but as late as last summer they were handing out hits like time was the cheapest commodity going.

Charlie got hit with five and was expecting only two; he'd kept a perfect record, which meant suppressing a heartfelt urge to pound a few motherfuckers in the face. Church attendance was regular—he stopped just short of joining the choir. It was full of fags and Nazis, anyway. Now it was better, but now they'd smacked him with five and the kindly advice: "Don't worry, son—you'll get out of here someday." Charlie was pretty mean for a while, told everybody on this end of the gallery just who was boss. Nobody argued with him—it was really a lousy break.

One guy in B-Block supposedly got hit with ten years. "Bring back ten and we'll talk again." How could anybody say that to anyone with a straight face? Even the inmates were laughing, it was so outrageous.

But these people have practically unlimited power, and the whole thing amounts to just another trial. What they want to know about is the crimes you weren't convicted for, a few statements that amount to a confession, and anything else you'd care to tell them—make it easy on yourself. A lot of shit goes on behind those closed hearing-room doors, you can bet.

How to face it? The best advice I can get from anyone comes from big Mack, the light-fingered Irishman who commands Cell Study with a quiet sneer: "Just answer their questions as briefly as you can, say Thank You, and get out." Mack has had a lot of experience at these things—he's right more often than wrong. But some of the stories about parole hearings are fairly hair-raising.

What's on trial is your life, and they really believe they have the whole story right there, in their very private dossiers. You are one guilty son of a bitch, that's for sure. Guilty as sin, and you better show some contrition. Not too much, they'll think you're pulling too hard.

They know a man knows when he's ready. Only sometimes he might know this too well, and that's bad, too. You've got to remember, how you hit a particular case affects other cases, too; affects the whole system. The system is what we're here to uphold. Some of these birds might have legitimate complaints, but when you look at the total picture, they don't mean anything. If any of them were really a good risk, they wouldn't be in here— right? "All one-hundred-percent failures," the executive commissioner agrees, patting his Legionnaire button. "We do the best we can." It would really be a disfavor to everyone concerned to go easy on them. If you make a mistake, it gets top headlines: "TWO-WEEK PAROLEE KILLS FIVE!" But let's not think about that. Let's hand out this time and get out of here; this particular prison always gives me the creeps . . .

After the thing at Auburn, they started giving lighter hits here, a few "breaks." No doubt out of a sense that things have to move a little faster—the Tombs riots indicate another avalanche of prisoners, and the seams are already close to bursting; got to make room . . .

To say I'm not nervous would be something less than true. A lurking evil in this place keeps me wanting to think about other things, or not to think at all. To fan the flame of consciousness in here is to risk the fire of delirium. Sometimes I see it, the troopers or guards advancing with their guns at hip level, pumping away; the blood, the cries, the utter desolation. It's a vision that comes and goes, but that can be the only outcome when communications finally break down completely. The authorities aren't coping with the problem; they're staying aloof, making their minor changes through paper work, directives.

What these men want is somebody to talk to them, some sign there are real human beings somewhere at the helm. You could pass a thousand new laws, it wouldn't make any difference. They know that laws and rules and regulations are never any better than the people administering them. But you have to start somewhere . . .

Lists of demands have been circulating around the blocks, seeking general inmate approval. Sam probably did some, but he's not the only one. Brother Irving has been working through the courts, slowly and painfully and persistently, to get certain regulations changed, and it looks like he's about to succeed. Rumor has it we're going to be allowed to send sealed, uncensored letters to lawyers and government officials.

A revolutionary notion, if you have some faith left in government officials. It's really an amazing thing. Brother Irving is a radical black, small, dark, smooth-scalped, with a sly, intelligent smile. He didn't like me at all at first, but he signed up for the Sociology Seminar I managed to get started. I don't know if I'd trust him, there's a certain coldness in his approach to things, but I have to admire his guts in remaining an individual despite his other affiliations. This is what makes him powerful, able to get things done. "When it comes right down to it, it's us acting as individuals that can cause any change in the system, working within it. But you've got to be able to pursue an idea, to take it all the way, to fight for it on an individual basis."

Fucking brilliant—there aren't too many leaders, black or white, who see this. The real issue is between society and the individual—race is an issue convenient to those who would obfuscate this fact. And most people would rather not have it, which is why they are born followers. It takes everything an individual has to become one; some of his power is always lost when he yields identity to a group. Government still operates on the principle of expediency, and it is only the individual who can confront this, who has the power of conscious decision to do or not do something about the quality of his life under conditions of oppressive authoritarianism· Self-respect can never be given from without, it can only be developed from within. Oppression offers for too many an excuse for searching for it among the images projected by ideological groups. Which is why we lead such highly symbolic lives, thrice removed from ourselves by layers of image-response conditioned into us practically from the cradle.

It may be true that we are nothing but images of the Creator. Allah; the Divinity; the Universal Mind—the Supreme Being. But then that is what we should contemplate.

There might be such a thing as grace, and it might be very much like the ability to act without fretting over the possible perfections or imperfections of the outcome. This trip through mortality needs a guide, there's no doubt about it. But how are we going to get in contact except through ourselves? If one molecule of protein contains all the riddles in the universe, it probably contains also all the answers. But the vision we need to see that molecule may be more than physical science has yet had to offer.

On the level of human affairs it seems to me that dialectical materialism never does anything more than describe a material process. The evolution of the universe is perhaps eternal, but history is what we see, and the more we contemplate it, the more evidence piles up of human madness. I don't see how we can escape the trap without going beyond the realm of the material, whatever else we may do. But our leaders, even those officially involved with religion, do nothing but leave the field open for all the satanists and other shoddy occultists. Maybe they're afraid to infringe upon the power of the devil.

In which case, let us pray for them no matter what they have done. Their crimes have yet to be paid for.

The headstand posture has much to recommend it, but you can overdo it if you're not careful. Done just right, with effort but without excess, it can cause a positive glow afterward, a feeling of well-being that keeps back the cold and adds color to the face. Concentration becomes significantly more possible; eventually you may alter your relationship with everything around you.

It can make you fast or slow, depending on the speed ,ou need. But at least it's natural speed, a rarity in these days. Secret plots abound, but as a rule I turn deaf ears to them. I'm a short-timer and they know it, so it's okay.

Nothing elaborate, really. Take over the prison and try to win a few demands.

It's breezy to say, easy to figure out. But there's hell in it, and I'd just as soon be struck dumb as to say something wrong.

Because it's no longer a case of black takeover. By and large it would happen that way, anyway—but the complexion of any governing body in this prison would have to be only one color: gray.

In a year it's changed. The young blacks aren't all militants, some of them smoked grass with Whitey, some of them screwed the best pussy in Nyack and West Scarsdale without having to wipe their feet on the back porch.

These are the real revolutionaries—the ones who'd prefer to fuck without a vengeance. White pussy in the streets was common; if you waited, it would come to you wrapped in furs. All you had to do was take the ribbon from her hair and turn it loose. But you really couldn't see wasting all the in-laws, future ones that is, if you both kept on and didn't get busted, as they were nice enough to keep you coming over frequently, and her little sister was the biggest tease in town.

The only time you thought about being a nigger was when the cops buzzed you for no reason, walking home late those summer nights. It made you surly, and since they couldn't touch you without offending some very good neighbors, they waited.

"Educated nigger," they said. "We'll have to show him by the book."

And so forth.

Pussy isn't really the problem, just a symptom. The country has more than enough to go around, and if anyone's hurting, it's because he hasn't really heard the news —it's a free country. Of course, there are certain preserves, but that's merely a matter of money protecting money. The wealthy girls who invented Women's Lib might really have been looking for a way to meet men other than under the counter. Otherwise, we can only suspect another tedious CIA plot, another spoke in the wheel whose job it is to grind the American male into appropriate consistencies of corporate gristle.

I swear to God, we had some for lunch this noon.

Ron is very beautiful. Brains like quicksilver, yet he prefers to remain in the metal shop. They shipped him there for punishment, and he turned it into a deal. Twenty-one, black, suburban New York, busted for acid, grass, and related foolishness. When we rap, the rest of Cell Study dissolves from the conscious mind, leaving only dull smudges.

"Hey man, what'cha been doing?"

"Writing poetry. Want to read some?"

"No, I just came up here to shoot the shit for a while. I hear you're up for the Board this week."

"That's right."

217

"No sweat, but you've got to find a job."

"I know it. That's the drag."

"You sending out letters?"

"Sure. The ones I get back say business is bad right now, try later."

"Drag. I'll give you the names of some people I know. Make me a cup of coffee."

So I start reading my poetry anyway, and it cracks him up. Almost anything does, and pretty soon this cracks me up. He wears his good spirits under a frown of gloom. This place has damn near bugged him out, but he'll never admit it.

Never.

The Admiral smoked a curved briar and used it to good effect in punctuating his questions with the accusative.

"Just answer the questions Yes or No, answer all questions, please. Did you sell drugs?"

"I pleaded guilty to the charge of Possession of a Dangerous Drug. The sale—"

"Just Yes or No, please. Did you sell drugs?"

"In my estimation there was no legitimate—"

"We're not asking you about that. We want to know if there was an agent, and you gave him something, and he gave you some money in return. Yes or no."

"Yes."

"Have you used drugs?"

"Yes." Short and simple, let's get out of here. F. Lee Bailey couldn't do a thing with this.

It's murder. "LSD, marijuana, hashish."

"Hmm. What started you on drugs?"

"Well, I went to see this ear, nose, and throat specialist on Long Island seven or eight years ago. I had a persistent bronchial complaint, upper-respiratory infections, the like. Anyway, he put me on these pills called Daprycyl, which I later found out were a combination of dextroamphetamine, phenobarbital, and aspirin."

"Goofballs," the Spanish-looking guy on the right, a recent appointee, says. The one in the middle remains silent and is invisible except for the gleam of his glasses. He may be God.

"Well, and how long did you take these—goofballs —Mr. Coons?"

"I had a renewable prescription which I kept going for two years. I was pretty sick after that and started to get into the other stuff for relief."

Back to the Admiral. "Well, Mr. Coons, do you believe all this—incarceration—was really necessary?"

It's such an unbelievable question I don't answer. I just blink at him, stunned. Was he really asking me that? Some faint sense of embarrassment for him made me squirm in my seat.

He let it ride but soon got tough again. He bawled me out, his partner tossed in some remarks about possible sexual deviation (some ex-girlfriend must have squealed) just to let me know they had a lot more in their dossier than they needed to show, enough to keep me in jail for life, in fact, and then it was all over and I said "Thank you" and left.

The hack outside the door, an officer, looked sympathetic. There are such hacks and they do have such feelings. Maybe I was a little ashen from having just been put through the grinder. All my witty remarks and clever, not to mention enlightening, explanations had faded away on me in there. These people were efficient and assured of their power—they wouldn't hesitate to crush you like a bug. But more than that, the atmosphere of a hearing room lends about as much to the possibility of expansive and imaginative discourse as the average butcher shop.

"We'll let you know," the Admiral said at the end. Don't call us, we'll call you. It's hard getting used to the idea of being a criminal, but once you see them fingering the plump folder with your name on it and your history inside, it all becomes very official. Cut and dried, as they say.

MARCH

This is the day I'm supposed to be going home. The Board gave me the date, but regular parole is contingent upon obtaining assurance of employment from the outside *before* they let you out the door. So far, the only answers I've gotten to job letters say just about the same thing: Things are tough, see us later—like when you get out.

So it's Catch-22 again. "State law," my P.O. keeps explaining, "says you're required to have a job before you go out."

"What about Reasonable Assurance?"

"That's something they use when there's a depression."

So it was Nixon who was keeping me in, by naming it a recession. But the P.O. was lying, because I happen to know five guys, all black, getting out this very week with no damn job assurance at all. A college education really works against you in prison. Not much sympathy from civil-service clerks who came up the hard way—by marrying Big Brother.

Meanwhile Big Mack's on his way out the door on Conditional Release and is looking very satisfied with himself. Sam's back in Cell Study, or at least the school—they seem to have him just sort of wandering around the place, sometimes with guitar. He came up today and did a few Beatles things.

The Reverend —————— has lost control and is trying to cover it up with additional paper work, which only makes everybody more bugged than ever with him. Really an affable chap, but his mind, when it isn't pinned down to the printed memo, has a tendency to wander all over the place. The rest of the time he spends trying to figure out who's plotting against him this week. He and Officer O'Sullivan, who sits outside in the hall, don't get along.

I really haven't much enthusiasm for writing any more —maybe they've cured me. The Cured Writer is a familiar figure on the American landscape, as William Burroughs well knew when he wrote *Naked Lunch*. Sort of a cured novel, although no doubt a work of genius, at least by comparison with what's been around.

He was at least the first one to see totalitarianism from a chemicological point of view. Quite a picture, and you don't have to really look through the eye of a needle to see it. People are beginning to hallucinate off nothing, I suspect. Brain Damage is packaged and sold over the counter and sung about in the average TV commercial.

I can't get away from them during the day because the yard TV's right under our window, and most of those gophers packed around it are deaf. Saturdays and Sundays are especially bad.

But I'm a short-timer now, so I walk around the yard with the lingering feeling that something might happen before I get out. Something bad.

The warm weather brings forth a new manner of life. Militant groups of blacks and Puerto Ricans are jogging and training and doing their exercises like they were headed for the next Olympics. And they're beginning to rid the City and downstate joints of some of the hard-core guerrillas; already some are filtering in here, though not especially in D-Block yet.

Meanwhile there's softball and I almost got on a team. Name of the Playboys, a bunch of psychedelic castoffs who banded together for purposes of presenting a more or less united front to the block. It's amazing to watch them play. They're so bad, the other teams can't believe it, and consequently lose to them. I held out for pitcher, touting my "floater," a slow ball that arcs high and sometimes doesn't even come down. "I threw one up in '67," I tell them, "and it's still going around up there, the Russians trying to figure out what new menace in the way of satellites we've put up." They didn't buy it, not the team but the manager—a dumb ginzo named Vinnie who's never even smoked a reefer. Claims he went to a party and someone slipped acid in his wine, causing him to go berserk and slice a dude to pieces. Sure. Some head. I suppose the judge bought the story, too. Anything to explain the monstrosities of the sick human psyche, so long as it doesn't infringe on our basic right to be nasty mean-ass sons of bitches.

The Psychedelic Sad Sacks, they should have called themselves. Because they got caught. There's nothing sadder than that.

Guys are already coming up to me and saying: "What, you still here? I thought you made the Board, man!"

It's really embarrassing and will probably get worse. I have no job prospects at all, and my energy level is in another down slump. The letters I write are often as not plain ridiculous:

Dear Sir:

As you may note from the official letterhead given me by this institution, you are dealing with someone who has journeyed somewhat past the pale.

However, things are looking up; this is no longer a prison, it's a State Correctional Facility, which if it makes me less of a criminal is all to the good, as I really need a job to get out of here and will expect your answer by return mail, if not sooner.

Respectfully,
Mad Dog Coll

Or

Sir:

Have you ever considered the risks you are taking by hiring people who've never been to prison? Pause, then, for some edification on this subject.

An ex-con is a person whose personal history has been thoroughly documented, and everything can be held against him. Consequently, there are few better security risks around. These other people off the streets, with their degrees and all—why you just never know what they might do. They might dip their fingers in honey, they might freak out and chew holes in your wall-to-wall carpeting.

An ex-convict at least is toilet-trained. He knows exactly when to flush, refraining from permitting his fecal matter to float around to the point where odious vibrations may be felt in far-flung reaches of the massive shithouse he has been trained to shit in.

There are many more fine points to be mentioned, but first I would like to hear from you.

Very truly yours,
Archie Bunker

But it's really a losing game, if you play it the way they say. First of all the prospective employer is put off by a letter obviously from a prison, and we don't really have time for that. Then, if in a stray moment he opens it, sniffs it, and decides it isn't lethal, he may read it. Or his secretary, or the night janitor, or somebody.

Let's say he reads it. Let's say the con who wrote it took a few Cell Study courses in English and can almost write. Or let's say he paid somebody two packs of Pall Malls to write it for him.

To skip a lot of shit, the employer is one in a million and decides to hire the guy, out of the goodness of his heart, out of belief that the quality of mercy is not strained, that God is not dead but may appear onstage at the Fillmore East any day now; out of sheer desperation, perhaps, over the fact that his own life seems as though it's being lived in a prison sometimes, so maybe it would help if for once he gave some poor sucker a halfway even break.

Now he's got the Department of Parole to contend with. They'll ring him up ere long and start some kind of a phone rap:

"Mr. Blivitsky?"

"Speaking."

"Jones of the State Parole Department. We believe a letter was sent to you by one of our lunatic assassins, a punk named Smith."

"That's right. I answered it last week—no, ten days ago. When you letting the—when you letting Smith out? I got lots of work, but can't afford to hold vacancies open."

"We understand, of course, Mr. Blivitsky, which is exactly why we're calling you. As you know, we make every effort to protect the public from Crime, as perpetrated largely by known criminals, especially those wily ones who have somehow escaped the scrupulous attention and thoroughgoing screening given everyone by our State Parole Board. [He pauses to clear his throat.] Now, concerning this Smith, we can't say we'd exactly recommend him, but then it's true the man could use whatever help you're able to offer. Alcoholic, you know. Is the job a sensitive one?"

"Nah, assistant night janitor is all."

"Aha! I see! Well, Smith isn't so bad, I don't mean to paint you a really bad picture, our correctional facilities are the finest in the land. However, I would make sure no pens or blank checkbooks are left in unlocked drawers . . ."

By this time Blivitsky is a little bit sad about the whole idea. When Jones begins telling him about the forms he must fill out, he suddenly remembers a late luncheon date and promises to call back sometime.

And perhaps a little bit grateful to Jones and the Department of Parole for having saved him from a confrontation with Public Enemy Number One.

But it's not always such a laughing matter.

Not usually, in fact.

APRIL

No job. Old friends are few, and can't come through. When they write, they say things are tough, look us up later.

When you get out.

They've got the key, but they can't or don't want to use it. There are still dollars to be shook from the war-decimated bushes. There are plays to go to, movies to see, songs to sing, girls to screw, and girls to make love to. Choices to make: What shall I do with my afternoon? Let's see if the buds are out in the park yet.

Too busy, too tired, too torn, too troubled. You can't blame them, either. Most of them got sucked into being what they are, just as you got sucked into being in here. As the Gay Lib Front no doubt puts it, one good suck deserves another. But it makes writing letters boring, so to hell with it. Maybe we'll get to see a riot yet. If we can't get to the world, maybe the world will come to Attica.

Someday. In the meantime we can only go through these last days like a spectator in Pompeii who has come to see the sights, hoping they dated his ticket right.

Some days are quite warm, and the yard gang gets it quick in shape so the does and the deer can frolic. Struttin' with some barbecue, Mr. G. gives me a rare wave and a smile. I wish I wouldn't worry him so much, but I don't know how not to. He's hardly spoken to me since New Year's, when we had that murderous argument. I was totally unprepared for it and didn't do a damn thing to help him understand my point of view. He thinks I'm something like an overage James Dean with permanent acne scars and a mind cooked out by hellish White Acid, at times. He's really afraid of that shit, because somebody said it takes you into your mind. No thanks, none of that.

So he reads his books on the Navy in World War II and only takes potshots when necessary.

Often past me, but at me just the same.

"Hey, Ralph!"

"Yeah, Mr. G.?"

"It says here in the paper that LSD is a powerful hallucinogen which in its pure form can cause psychic contamination and even brain damage on mere contact."

"No shit, Mr. G.?"

I squirm and decide to bite. "It's worse than that, Mr. G.," I interject. "Even to *rap* with anybody who's been contaminated by it can send you off on a trip."

Since then, we don't rap too much.

Her (Conclusion)

Sometimes when the music stopped and you could hear the band tuning up for the next set, her head would stir on my shoulder. She'd look up at me with her Indian-brown eyes as though wanting me to give some signal.

I knew I was being too slow, but it was only because I wanted every moment to last forever. This was the nature of my insanity then—to think there was a way to beat Time.

Well, I won't go into the raucous scenes. The riot of her in my blood was enough to leave scars. But with her, nothing was really operative without the *dinero*. She didn't quite know this herself, otherwise she'd have had to contend with those feelings that can't be defined in the pages of Love Comics.

I knew that, too. But shit.

MAY

Air of menace mixed with almost festive gaiety. Contradictions abound. The yard is full of springtime activity, but some of these restless stirrings have more dubious implications.

The place is split right down the middle. Half would go for some action in the near future if somebody strong enough persuaded them; the other half still believe relief may yet come through the courts and legislators, via writs and appeals and letters to congressmen and the governor. Relative sanity seems on the latter side, but there's no monopoly. Anywhere. If anything, it's lacking just where it's needed most—at the top.

But then, real social mobility hasn't had anything to do with intelligence for quite some time, which may explain why we have become a nation of casualties. Even with money you might find yourself desperately lonely. Your desperation might be of such a quality and intensity as to drive you toward some irreversible act of love-in-reverse, and it might be the one time your friends can't fix it. In which case you might end up here and have to learn to live with the bitter realization that they may not even have wanted to. A nation of casualties needs its basket cases to give the rest a moderate sense of well-being.

But at the bottom they've had enough. Too many geniuses have been washed down the drainpipe of an ill-tempered economic system. Too many have ended up in insane asylums, their mad vibrations leaking out to destroy our dreams. Too much warpage and not enough woof.

Wait a minute. Why am I writing this? It's all been said before, and nobody listens. What I'd really like to do right now is listen to Bill Evans playing "Conversations with Myself." His dialectic is made of more than material stuff.

I want out.

ⅢⅢⅢⅢⅢ

To the bitter end, as they say—the people who say such things. The sure-thing job I had lined up with the state narcotics rehabilitation people fell through because of a sudden swift fall of the budget ax. They're laying off their own people; what on earth can they do for someone like me?

Nada. Maybe it's just as well, but it seemed like the ticket home. Now I have to wait till the end of June, my Conditional Release date. They present it to you as a contract. You don't have to sign it, it's full of bond-slave clauses, but then you don't have to go home, either. You can bring it *all* back if you want to. It's a free country.

The deal is, you can sign and go home after two thirds of your sentence has been served. But unlike parole, your time in the streets doesn't count. Which means you'll have the remainder of your sentence to do regardless of when they pick you up and decide they want you back. Every other state with a Conditional Release setup has dropped the noxious practice of stopping time except this one. But New York is the Empire State, and no empire can be maintained without a few slaves.

It's getting better, my P.O. assures me. "They're dropping some of the pettier rules," he says. I certainly hope so. It might make some allowance for the hand of God, now and then.

And it probably is getting better, somehow, somewhere, but the rate at which they're projecting improvements only reveals the nature of the leviathan. You could die in its stomach before it ever decides to yawn.

The Steel Whale. If its jaws don't open a bit, somebody's going to start lighting fires, that's for sure. Real soon, too.

234

ⅬⅬⅬⅬⅬⅬ

This is the longest month of my bit. I can't even look at the calendar. I can't believe the numbers have anything to do with the days, or the days with the numbers. I've given up writing job letters because I can't believe there are jobs, at least not ones I could do for more than a week. Maybe they've broken me down—it's hard to tell sometimes in here what's broken down and what isn't—but I still don't plan to become a factory worker again. I've had enough of that to last several lifetimes.

What I feel is mainly exhaustion and a fear of further exhaustion. Somehow I'll get the energy up to do something, I know it—but it won't come to me till I walk out the door. My eyes are weary of this place.

Still, they see. Impatience is the mood, and the way they're diddling around with the little details of regulations actually only makes matters rather worse. It makes the against-the-wall people nervous, louder, and more articulate in their demands—this is no time for tinkering. What's needed is a change in basic approach, an identity of prison reform with social reform, which in turn requires general admission from the top that we are *all* pretty sick. To try to assert otherwise is madness, but they're still doing it, still defending the Perfect Society. Maybe there are some good men in Corrections. God help them. Their job is a lot bigger than they know; it really starts outside these walls.

Some of these people should be off the streets, but some of the streets should be off the map.

It's as simple as that.

JUNE

I'll take the Main Drag anytime, and it's just like the song says. There's Broadway and Seventh Avenue, there's Broadway and Seventy-ninth Street. There may be a whole lot of Broadways in the world, but there's only one Broadway. I want it. No more slow death in back-country towns and cities. If New York is falling through, I'll go with it, because that's where it is.

Not so much the bright lights as the people. They're used to all forms of insanity, including quite often their own. They operate little luncheonettes and aren't afraid to brag about the freshness of their eggs and bacon. They tend bar or hang out, because when it comes right down to it, they like to be around people. They go through their changes faster, and recover faster. When they're sick, they hole up, when they're mad, they go to Bellevue, when they're broke they scheme or go on relief, when they've got something going, they'll buy you a drink.

People are nice everywhere, but it's hard for them to remember that. They've been through too much, and they don't feel connected with anything, which would make even a dog mean and surly. But the hate side of the coin can't come up every time, and if there's anything left, it'll be along Broadway. Back to Nature is a wound-licking proposition. Walden probably exists more in some off-Broadway hotel room than it does in the Massachusetts woods. It was nothing but an idea anyway, never any better than the individual who pursues it.

Maybe this time I'll see them coming, the dealers with nothing to sell, the free-trippers who'd like to take you for a ride. As for the prophets of Apocalypse, I don't deny them, but I've got to live this life.

Just give me strength.

Coons
ATTICA DIARY

DATE DUE

AG 2 73		
SF 21 73		
NO 2 73		
NO 30 74		
MR 1 '77		
AUG 3 78		
JAN 4 79		
APR 18 80		
JE 20 84		